Face The Music

She found the courage to face her past
and change her future

ANTONIETA MITCHELL

Face The Music

She found the courage to face her past
and change her future

ANTONIETA MITCHELL

T&J Publishers

A SMALL INDEPENDENT PUBLISHER WITH A BIG VOICE

Printed in the United States of America by
T&J Publishers (Atlanta, GA.)
www.TandJPublishers.com

© Copyright 2022 by Antonieta Mitchell

All rights reserved. This book or parts thereof may not be reproduced in any form, stored in a retrieval system, or transmitted in any form by any means-electronic, mechanical, photocopy, recording, or otherwise-without prior written permission of the author, except as provided by United States of America copyright law.

Cover Design by Timothy Flemming, Jr. (T&J Publishers)
Book Format/Layout by Timothy Flemming, Jr. (T&J Publishers)

ISBN: 979-8-218-01701-9

To contact author, go to:
Facebook: FaceTheMusic56
Instagram: @ _facethemusic
Email: FaceTheMusic56@gmail.com

I dedicate this book to my children who inspired me and gave me the courage to write it and speak about my experience. They said, "Ma, you need to tell your story." And that's why I wrote this book. Thank you and I love you all.

I would love to thank God for putting it on my daughter Fatimah's heart to help me get this book published.

I would love to dedicate this book to my readers because they are the ones that will most benefit from it. I hope that whomever reads it will discover how to *Face The Music* as I have and come out on top.

> "Healing takes courage, and we all have courage, even if we have to dig a little to find it."
> —Tori Amos

TABLE OF CONTENTS

Chapter 1:	Sunny Days	11
Chapter 2:	Dark Secrets	19
Chapter 3:	Just Like Cinderella	29
Chapter 4:	Around The Block	39
Chapter 5:	Screwed	49
Chapter 6:	Lost And Found	61
Chapter 7:	Strange Visitors	71
Chapter 8:	Craziness	79
Chapter 9:	The Bastard Out Of Brooklyn	93
Chapter 10:	The Scariest Day Of My Life	103
Chapter 11:	Emancipation	113
Chapter 12:	Closure	125

Chapter 1
SUNNY DAYS

I WAS BORN ON JUNE 2, 1968, IN THE REPUBLIC OF Panama, which is known for its pristine beaches and its gorgeous mixture of modern and colonial architecture. It's referred to by many as the jewel of Central America. But I have very few memories there because I didn't remain there for long. When I was just five-years-old, I moved from Panama to the United States of America to live with my mom and siblings in Brooklyn, New York.

In New York, we lived in project housing. Life in the projects was fun. There was always something interesting taking place. My siblings and I spent most of our time outside, running all over the neighborhood with our friends. We did all kinds of wild and crazy things together. We had a large field next to our apartments where the older guys would often go to play football. We treated those games like they were big money events, cheering on the players like they were professional athletes. Those were always great to watch.

FACE THE MUSIC

We played the boyfriend-girlfriend game like all kids. There was one boy I had big crush on; his name was Ronnie. I spent a lot of time crying over him. I can't recall why. But whenever I felt sad or disappointed, I would turn to Sonya, my best friend, for support. She probably got tired of hearing me talk about him all the time; or maybe not. Either way, I loved talking to her because she was a good listener, she was my confidant.

After a while, things started getting weird between us. Sonya started acting strange. At first, she was cool. She would listen to me, let me cry on her shoulder, give me advice, and then we would go on to do fun stuff. But now, she began acting like she wanted more from me than I was willing to give. I guess her devotion came at a price.

One day, while I was venting to her about Ronnie, without warning, she simply leaned over and kissed me. As she kissed me, I felt confused; the whole situation felt awkward. I was only around ten or eleven-years-old, still very much naive concerning the way of the world. I didn't know what was happening or what she was doing, and maybe she didn't know either. Maybe she was experimenting, trying something she had witnessed somewhere else. Perhaps it was just her curiosity getting the better of her. Or maybe she really liked me like that. All I knew is that wasn't for me. I didn't like it. Afterwards, I began to avoid her and I made sure not to be alone with her anymore.

Our apartment was packed to the brim like sardines in a can. Aside from mom and dad living there, I had nine sisters and three brothers who shared that living space. As you can imagine, there was hardly a dull moment there. You

CHAPTER 1: SUNNY DAYS

would hear on a regular basis yelling, arguing, fighting and crying. Our parents spent plenty of time breaking up fights over the television set. And don't let one of us stay in the restroom too long. But despite the conflicts, having a huge family was wonderful. Making jokes around the dinner table, watching movies together in the den, eagerly waiting for hand-me-downs and all of the other things associated with big families, that's what made childhood memorable. Sleeping in one bed with several siblings, smelling one another's funky feet and tussling over the covers, all hallmarks of a robust household. We knew each other well—we had no other choice but to. Our love was palpable, genuine. We were tight knit like a gang. If you messed with one of us, you messed with all of us. We got on each other's nerves a lot, but we wouldn't allow others to screw with family.

Again, we lived in the projects, so we definitely weren't rich. We epitomized the phrase "humble beginnings." I'm actually glad we did because I think a huge house would have pulled us apart more than anything. Everyone having their own bedroom and bed, we would not have gotten to know each other as much. Although financially limited, we were rich in other ways. We were rich in relationships. We were rich in creativity—we had to make up games and play pretend. Whatever we could find—a tire, sticks and other items laying around—we turned into swords, spears, light sabers, magic wands, and more. When you don't have money, you have to get used to exploring using your imagination.

One time, one of my sisters tried to scare me. She had me doing the whole "Bloody Mary" thing—you know, where you stand in front of a mirror and chant "Blood Mary"

13

over and over until her apparition appears. That didn't scare me because I didn't believe that was real. So I didn't think anything of it. However, there was one thing that terrified me: we watched a movie that was popular at the time—and still is. That movie is arguably one of the scariest films of all times: The Exorcist.

For six-months after watching that film, I could hardly sleep. I had nightmares. I grew paranoid, hearing and seeing things, strange things. There is one incident that, until this day, I am convinced happened, although none of my family and friends believed me: I witnessed a toy truck move on its own across my bedroom floor. It happened!

To this day, I still have trouble sleeping in the dark, especially with a closet open—I get the funny feeling that something is staring at me. All of this started after looking at that darn movie. Needless to say, I never looked at that movie again, nor any film like it.

*

My parents were hard workers. My mom was a caretaker, looking after elderly patients. My dad was a transmission specialist with his own shop. Because they worked long hours, my siblings and I had to look after each. We did most of the cooking around the house. We cleaned a lot. We had to run to each other's rescue whenever problems arose, and this wasn't always pleasant; this required sacrificial love like the time when one of my sisters was calling out for help from the restroom. Hearing her pleas, I rushed into the restroom to see what was going on. She was panicky and distraught because her bowels weren't moving. I had to examined her

CHAPTER 1: SUNNY DAYS

bottom, and that's when I noticed it: a long worm dangling from her rectum. Talk about a test of love, I had to get down and pull that worm out of her. Yuck! But that's what family is for.

My parents loved to entertain and throw parties. They lived for this. They loved music and played it constantly throughout the apartment. They would lose themselves in the tunes of R&B, the golden oldies, and the festive sounds of Latin beats.

We constantly had house-parties. As kids, my siblings and I were usually sent to our rooms, but the loud music and ruckus carried through the walls. I would peep my head out of the door and see familiar faces—some faces weren't so familiar. Adults retreated into a cloud of smoke while gulping down beer and other drinks; some staring intensely at a hand of cards. My siblings and I usually found ourselves asleep before the party could end. We couldn't keep up.

Music was our escape. We were a musical family. Now, we weren't performers like the Jackson Five; we just laughed and danced to it, chilled and relaxed to it. It massaged the stress of the day out of our minds. Naturally, I became a music lover. I would sway to its sounds like a person drifting on the ocean being rocked by its waves. I would drift into a state of ecstasy and lose track of time. Yeah, it was that intense; this became one of my defining characteristics.

CARELESS WHISPERS

A slow dance changed my life. Let me explain. It started when I met a boy named Lester. There were few guys who could compete with my love of music. If I messed with a boy, he had to love music just like me. That's how we connected. Also, he had to have nice hair. That's one of the things that attracted me to Lester. He was cute with beautiful, curly hair, and he loved music as much as I did.

Lester had a good head on his shoulders, and his parents were wonderful people. They were always kind to me, and treated me like one of their own. Lester was special because he was the first guy I had ever slow-danced with. That was a magical experience to me; it was breathtaking. We danced alone in his living room to the song "Careless Whispers" by George Michael. He knew how to make a girl feel special.

The flames of teenage lust raged like a wildfire, causing us to land in the bedroom. He was my first. My first time having sex, my heart was beating like crazy. I was so nervous, but Lester was calm and gentle. Or at least, he pretended to know what he was doing.

Like the typical meme, everything seemed like paradise until the morning time came—and by morning, I'm talking about real life. As we all know, sex can lead to things like pregnancy. That was what happened to me. I didn't detect anything right away, but then I missed my period.

Immediately, I went to a free clinic to see if I was pregnant. My suspicions were confirmed: I was pregnant. And there was no doubt in my mind who the father was. When I told Lester, his response was less than charming. He started denying that it was his child. He claimed that he couldn't have been the father since we only did it once. I was wondering where that guy was who slow danced, caressed

CHAPTER 1: SUNNY DAYS

and finessed me so gently. I wanted to know where that compassionate lover went. He flipped on me. He turned into another person after I gave him the news.

I understand now that he was simply scared, but so was I; however, I was willing and ready to handle my responsibility. It didn't matter how much he grumbled, complained, denied and bucked at the truth, I was sticking to my guns and reminded him at every turn that the baby was his. He just had to get used to it; after all, he was ready and all too anxious for sex. Why not its consequences?

Although Lester was in denial, his parents weren't. They accepted the baby right away. They were supportive of me throughout my entire pregnancy, making sure that I had everything I needed. They were actually excited about the arrival of the newborn. Eventually, Lester came around; it took him a moment, though. I think what got him was the moment he stepped into the hospital room after I had given birth and looked at the baby for the first time. Those little eyes staring back at him melted his heart, and from that moment, he was thoroughly convinced that it was his baby. I could see a new light in his eyes.

This is where my life took an interesting turn. This is where the storm clouds rolled in. This is where a few deep, dark secrets began to come to the surface and skeletons started coming out of the closet, and I'm talking about skeletons in my own family. It all started with the birth of my son.

*

Lester's family was incredibly supportive of me and the baby.

They would buy pampers, milk, and other essentials for the baby. It warmed my heart to witness them cradle the baby in their arms while singing to him; the joy in their souls beaming as bright as the smiles on their faces. Although Lester and I broke after I had our son—you know the saying, "Boys will be boys"—he was still active in our baby's life. He played his part. But the real stars of the show were his parents. They did everything for me and the baby. They unofficially adopted me as their own.

But I couldn't help but notice my parents wouldn't even lift a finger to do anything for me and the baby. That was odd. And I wanted to know why they were so cold and indifferent. I wasn't prepared for the answer I got.

Chapter 2
DARK SECRETS

I ALWAYS HAD A FEELING THAT MY PARENTS WERE HOLDING secrets from me. But to be fair, all parents conceal secrets when raising children; it's their tendency to withhold information when a child is too young to understand what's going on. I understood that much. However, there seemed to be a total lack of transparency in our home. My parents were good with covering up the dark underworld of hidden truths with music, parties, work and other things. We simply knew not to ask certain questions. But it wasn't long before I broke the cardinal rule and asked a question about my past that had been burning on my heart. This occurred when I was a little girl staying with my parents.

Like I mentioned in the previous chapter, I lived in The Republic of Panama for the first five years of my life. And although I didn't remember much from that time in my life, I would get occasional flashes of my time spent over there. I vaguely remembered certain faces. And like a mist or fog of obscurity that was slowly lifting, I was beginning to

FACE THE MUSIC

recall certain experiences that left me scarred from my time over there. The thing that triggered certain of my memories was an episode of *The Oprah Winfrey Show*.

At the time, Oprah produced a lot of shows dealing with the topic of childhood sexual abuse. She often pulled from her own childhood experiences where she experienced childhood sexual abuse at the hands of a family member. Her passion for the topic resonated through the television screen and penetrated my soul, invoking feelings of uneasiness within me. My heart rate would rise and I would feel cold chills and break out into sweats when listening to her talk about that subject. I felt panicky for some reason. And then the flashbacks came.

I remember sitting in the den watching Oprah, and she was dealing with the topic of sexual abuse. At that moment, I began having intense flashbacks to my time as a little girl in Panama. They were too unbearable, too heavy to dismiss. So I got up and went to my mom's room and asked her, "Mom, who was I living with in Panama?"

"You were living with your god-mother's parents. Why did you ask?"

"It's just I keep having these strange flashbacks. I think something may have happened to me while I was there."

"Something like what?"

"I might have been molested."

"Molested? What are you talking about? I don't know where you're getting that idea from!"

"I think it happened. In one of my flashbacks, I remember laying on top of a man—I guess it was grandpa. I

CHAPTER 2: DARK SECRETS

remember he had a beer-belly. We were in the bed together and he was doing something inappropriate."

"You know what I think? I think you're imagining things. Maybe you're spending too much time looking at television."

"No, I'm for real. I think I was molested. I can see it in my mind. I can remember it just a little bit." My mom got quiet. As I continued to talk, my memory was coming back to me. The bits and pieces that were obscured by the fog began to become clear to me. "I can remember being in a room with a man. I was laying in the bed with him, and then a woman came into the room." My mom just listened, but she didn't look too surprised. "I can remember when the woman came into the room, the man hid me under the covers so she wouldn't see me. And the crazy thing is there were other kids in the room with us. But for some reason, he had me lying on top of him in the bed. At one point, I think he had me performing oral sex on him."

After remaining silent, my mom finally spoke up, but her response left me feeling confused: "Look that was years ago. And it doesn't matter anyway because he's dead."

*

He's dead! That was the best she could offer me after I bore my heart to her and revealed to her a deeply traumatizing experience. That was tantamount to saying, Just forget everything! Just drop it and pretend like it never happened! I didn't know whether it was normal or not to be so indifferent and apathetic towards such a serious matter. Was it that I was being overdramatic? Was I simply digging up the past in an effort to gain pity for myself? Was it serious enough for me to bring up, or should I have just kept it inside and buried that secret in my soul? I felt invalidated, not knowing if I deserved to be heard and understood. Truthfully, I didn't know what and how to feel at that point, so I never brought it up again.

One thing became clear to me: My mom was hiding secrets from me. If she knew about grandpa and the type of man he was and either knew or suspected that he was doing bad things to me as a little girl, what else did she know? Were there any other incidents and occurrences from my past that she neglected to share with me, things that were effecting me in a major way? And if there were, could I trust her to tell me, to be truthful with me? Or would she simply blow off any and all concerns of mine as unimportant and downplay the emotions they invoke like she had just done?

Part of me wanted to shut up and be a good girl, and part of me wanted to probe my life further to find out more about my past. Part of me was curious about my mom and why she was so apathetic towards something I knew was serious, and part of me figured she felt it best to keep such secrets hidden to protect my heart. But the thing about trauma is it cannot be buried; it will control your life from a subconscious place. Memories I didn't even know I had resided inside of me, and they were the cause of some of my strange behaviors. Seeds of fear and suspicion were planted in me at an early age. Self-esteem issues and distrust of authority was also something planted in me as a child. And like every seed, these things will grow and blossom over time, becoming trees of negative behaviors.

CHAPTER 2: DARK SECRETS

There was always something in me that prevented me from feeling completely loved and accepted by my parents, especially my dad, Walter. I loved him, but I couldn't understand why I couldn't take to him like a loving daughter. I couldn't understand why there was such a hesitation inside of me when it came to him. In fact, I couldn't feel entirely free around both of my parents. I developed this uneasiness due to the words spoken to me by one of my sisters who lived with us. Just like me, she'd moved from Panama to live with us many years prior.

YOUR SISTER...FROM PANAMA

Her name was Carmen. She was much older than me, around thirty-years-old at the time. I was still very young. Carmen was a pretty cool person. I didn't really have any problems with her. But it was the small remarks she would throw my way that began to get to me. For example, she would always ask me, "You know you're adopted, right?"

I'm adopted! Who does this silly girl think she is? She doesn't know what she's talking about! I would dismiss her words and try to block them out of my head, thinking she was either messing with me, playing with me, or something like that, but there was a seriousness in Carmen's eyes whenever she'd talk about me being adopted. This disturbed me. I would get that tingly feeling that something wasn't right when she would tell me that, the same feeling I got while watching *The Oprah Winfrey Show*. I started to feel like I was being lied to again, like there were dark secrets swirling around my head like an ominous cloud.

I began questioning myself. Carmen's words were

getting to me; and not only hers, but other people's also. Other people would tell me I looked completely different from my siblings, like I didn't belong there. I felt like the ugly duckling. I grew more conscious of my appearance, noticing how different my hair looked, my skin complexion was from that of my siblings, how different my nose, my eyes, my cheekbones and other features looked. And the differences were noticeable. I didn't look like my siblings. But hey, I grew up with them. I lived with them. That was my family, so it didn't matter to me what I looked like. That was my attitude. And still is.

And yet, the seed of suspicion had been planted. My sense of identity was in jeopardy. I couldn't help but wonder what was going on. And my parents' actions didn't help much. They continued to treat me like differently from the rest of their kids, and even more after I had my son.

One of my sisters and I was pregnant at the same time. Lester's parents were more than accommodating to me and my baby, but I received zero support from my parents. They didn't buy pampers, wipes or powdered milk for the baby. There was no sense of joy and appreciation for my son's presence among them. But I did see joy on their faces while beholding my sister's baby. They would buy whatever she needed for her child. They would smile from ear to ear and sing beautifully while cradling her baby in their arms. I couldn't understand why. Why was my baby being treated different from my sister's?

Dad vowed to bestow upon any of his kids who provided him with his first grandson a special gift: a necklace he was saving as a family heirloom. I just knew I would receive

CHAPTER 2: DARK SECRETS

that gift, being that I was the first in the household to give birth to a boy. However, neither my son nor I received that necklace. He treated my son like he didn't count, which left me totally baffled.

ONE CRY

At first, I just thought my dad had a temper. He had a tendency to come down pretty tough on his kids when we stepped out of line. I can remember what he did to one of my sisters who was caught smoking cigarettes by a neighbor. When he found out about her smoking cigarettes, he waited for her to arrive home from school and then took her to the corner store to buy a pack of cigarettes. At first, his plan was to make her smoke the entire pack as punishment, but then he changed his mind and punished her by making her hold heavy jars of coins in each hand. He threatened that if she dropped one of the jars, he would beat her. Unfortunately, she dropped a jar and he beat her as promised. He had a reputation for being strict, but what I experienced at his hands when I was twelve-years-old was something beyond strictness.

 My dad sent me to the corner store to buy him a pack of cigarettes. My friend George walked to the store with me. While on our way to the store, we passed by a pizza restaurant that had an arcade inside of it. Like all kids, we were easily distracted and sidetracked. That arcade looked so fun. The flashy lights and digital sounds were so alluring. So we decided to go inside and play video games for a couple of minutes. Before we knew it, over an hour had passed, and I realized I still hadn't gone to the store to get the cigarettes.

FACE THE MUSIC

I rushed out of the arcade and got the cigarettes and then rushed back to the house, figuring he would be ticked off and probably yell at me for taking so long. I didn't expect what came next.

When I arrived home and went to give my dad the cigarettes, I could see the anger all over his face. My mom was sitting quietly on the bed. First, my dad asked me why did it take me so long. I didn't know what to tell him, so I just stared at him. I certainly wasn't going to confess that I was somewhere playing video games. Because I didn't answer him fast enough, he grabbed me and violently threw me against the wall and started beating me. He slapped me, struck me with objects, and threw me all over the room, from wall to wall. It was as if he hated me and wanted to beat the life out of me. It ended after he tossed me into his closet with such force that the shelves and all of the contents contained thereon came crashing down on me. My mom sat silently by and did and said nothing.

I was distraught. All I could do was cry. I cried and cried and cried, holding my body which was racked with pain. My sides hurt. My back hurt. My arms were throbbing. I could feel the sting on my face from his hand. Furthermore, my heart was crushed. But he wasn't done. He was like a locomotive filled with contempt, unable to stop. He wanted to finish me off. And the words he spoke were enough to do just that. "Why don't you just die! Just die so I can have one good cry and get it over with!"

Never before had he talked to anyone in our household like that. That anger and rage he demonstrated towards me wasn't normal; it had nothing to do with punishment;

CHAPTER 2: DARK SECRETS

that was deeply personal. But what had I done to him to make him hate me so much?

Looking back at it today, if he hated me, it would only make sense that he would also hate my son. He would want me to know he didn't approve of me and my son. Between his contemptuous attitude, mom's secretiveness, and Carmen's insistence that I didn't belong in our family, that I was the ugly duckling of the crew, I grew up feeling completely isolated and different. I grew up feeling like a stranger in my own home. And perhaps I was one. I was the oddball in the family, the one destined to bear the heavy weight of rejection. After a short while, this became painfully obvious to me, and it was this rejection that impacted my life in major ways, including how I saw myself.

FACE THE MUSIC

Chapter 3
JUST LIKE CINDERELLA

"**I CAN'T STAND YOU!**" I SHOUTED. "Well, I can't stand your little spoiled butt either," my uncle shouted back angrily. The two of us were going at it as if there was a ton of pent up anger waiting to burst out of me and onto him like the waters of a dam.

My uncle would stop by the house every Sunday to visit. Actually, he was my favorite uncle, and I believe in my heart that I was his favorite niece. That's what made our confrontation so strange to me. How things escalated from a simple visit to a huge argument between the two of us, I don't know, but it did. Furthermore, it seemed a little odd to me that a grown man would argue with a child to begin with. But there we were, at each others' throats in the presence of my mom and siblings.

"I wish you would just go somewhere!" I roared.

"Screw you! You know what? You're better off dead!" Those words uttered by my uncle pierced my heart like a poisoned arrow and left me stunned, at a lost for words.

"What the fuck did you just say?" I asked in total disbelief. Anger arose within me and I grabbed a butcher knife out of the kitchen drawer and then charged at my uncle. My mom intervened and wrestled the knife out of my hand.

All I could see was red. Rage had consumed me. My body shook uncontrollably, and I could practically taste blood at that moment. Those words were practically the same words my dad had just spoken to me a couple of nights prior. They wanted me dead!

It was as if I meant nothing to them. My dad, my uncle, neither of them cared about me as a person. And quite frankly, I questioned my mom's feelings towards me. The truth be told, my mom inflicted on me her own brand of abuse; she was also cruel, but she was very subtle with hers. She didn't curse me out with her words. She didn't say demeaning things to me. She maintained a Molly Ms. Practical persona, acting like an outside observer watching helplessly as her husband unleashed the wrath of the devil on me. But she was like the creature that takes small bites out of a person, nibbling on them slowly and subtly. Hers was a passive-aggressive assault. She would make me think I was the one that was crazy, I was the one with the problem; that's what made her abuse worse.

As a little girl, my hair was very long, silky, and wavy; it flowed all the way down to my butt. That hair was my pride and joy, a prized possession of mine. I was like Rapunzel, letting it hang at times, whipping it around for everyone to see. It made me feel beautiful, special. One day, I went to school with my hair hanging loosely but I returned home

CHAPTER 3: JUST LIKE CINDERELLA

with it in a ponytail. I didn't think anything of it, but this apparently angered my mom who accused me of allowing others to play with my hair. What she did next devastated me. She grabbed a pair of scissors and then cut my hair off. I was humiliated and embarrassed. I felt dehumanized. At that moment, I started to feel hatred rising inside of me. I hated my dad because of how he treated me, and now my mom because of her mistreatment of me, and not to mention the fact that she just stood there and watched quietly while my dad viciously beat me in her presence. Furthermore, she let my dad beat me while concealing the fact that he wasn't really my dad—that's what hurt me the most. I hated my uncle because of how he spoke to me. I was transforming into an angry young lady. I hated being at that house. I hated it! With a passion! The sight of that house was enough to cause panic and anxiety inside of me; it was as if a dark cloud hovered over our home insulating us in a bubble of negativity.

I was experiencing my own Cinderella story. I felt like an object of contempt within our household. Dad continued to cast subtle, contemptuous glances my way. I tried to avoid him as much as possible. My parents would make me clean the entire house by myself before I could do anything or go anywhere. My siblings were given menial, easy tasks. For example, one of my sisters was only tasked with cooking. I, on the other hand, had to clean the den, dining room, bedrooms, and the restrooms. If I didn't clean every room properly, I got punished for it; they would threaten to kick me out of the house. The worse part to me was cleaning the bathrooms. They had to be spotless. I had to scrub the toilets and showers and even the trash-cans clean. I would have to get on my hands and knees to reach those tough spots—they had to be cleaned thoroughly. I had to pick up behind everyone, flush behind them, wipe up behind them, and more. I started to feel like I was everyone's maid, which explains why even until this day I don't like to clean restrooms.

Tired of being mistreated, I finally gathered up the courage to run away from home. I believed that by doing this, my parents would come to their senses and treat me differently—treat me fairly and lovingly. I wanted them to stay up all night long, stressing and worrying over me, and realizing just how much they would miss me being around.

For two days, I was gone. I stayed at a friend's house—her parents didn't care that I was there. All I had to do was make up an excuse for being there and continue to go to school. I was sure my parents didn't know where I was. How could they? I didn't tell anyone where I was going. None of my siblings knew.

In my mind, I pictured my mom running around and pulling her hair out, wondering about my whereabouts. I wanted to punish her with my absence. I didn't expect too much out of my dad though. But at least mom would be worried sick about me, or so I thought. When I returned home, I told my parents I was kidnapped. I just wanted to see their reactions. I needed to know if they cared enough about me to shed tears over me, if it concerned them that I may have been lying in a ditch somewhere, hurt and alone, murdered, sold as a sex slave to a foreign diplomat overseas, abducted by aliens—anything! To be honest, the response I got from them wasn't what I was expecting: they didn't seem

CHAPTER 3: JUST LIKE CINDERELLA

too worried and concerned that I was missing. I would have expected my mom to be running all over town looking for me, going to all of my popular hangout spots, coming to my school, asking every neighbor in the community about my whereabouts and more, but neither of my parents went to such lengths to find me, and that cut me deep in my heart. Do they care about me at all? I wondered.

Crying myself to sleep became a nightly habit of mine. I couldn't bear the thought of not being loved or wanted by my parents. Some days, I stayed in the bed, overcome by a sense of numbness, unable to move. My legs would feel like cinderblocks, and my feet like they were stuck in quicksand. Every breath was difficult to intake. My chest would be filled with pain. At other times, my mind would be lost in a fog; crazy thoughts rummaging through my mind like a band of criminals. One thought that was constant in my mind was, It can't get worse than this. That's the hope I clung to in my soul. But right when I thought things couldn't get any lower, they did.

NOW I KNOW

The day was April 28, 1988. That beautiful day in spring I gave birth to my daughter, Melissa. She was a happy bundle of joy, an incredible spark of happiness in my life. Her father lived right across the street from me. We continued to have a relationship after Melissa's birth, but sadly, it didn't last long. We eventually broke up. However, he remained active in his daughter's life.

I still lived at home with my parents; not much had changed in that area. My mom still practiced what I call micro-aggressions: doing little mean and devious things to me out of anger and contempt. My dad was still cold and unwelcoming towards me for some unknown reason. I had simply learned to deal with it, to suppress what I felt and cope with it. In the meantime, I decided to seek love elsewhere. I held on to the fantasy of the perfect guy coming to rescue me and take me away from all of the chaos in my home. Such a classic fantasy, I know; a common tendency of those suffering from a deficiency of love and acceptance.

I was lonely, very lonely. My only real companion was music. Again, I'd wrap myself up in its airy arms and allow its rhythms to rock and sway me from side to side. That was my only real outlet, my only way to lose sight of my miseries and cares. But every now and then a good-looking guy would come along and steal my heart. And to be honest, guys didn't have to work hard to do that being that I was so wounded and vulnerable. I guess they could easily sense the emptiness in my heart. Perhaps desperation sat in my eyes. In either case, my quest for love took me down a dangerous and painful path, which I'll get into in a moment.

In our house, my bedroom was on the second level, next to the stairs. My parents' room was down the hall from mine. Taking care of a little baby meant I had to go back and forth from my bedroom to the kitchen downstairs often, usually throughout the night, warming up bottles of milk, throwing away soiled diapers and more.

One night, at around two in the morning, while heading downstairs to warm up some milk for the baby, I overheard my parents yelling from their bedroom. And they were loud, so loud, I could hear them clearly from the other

CHAPTER 3: JUST LIKE CINDERELLA

end of the hall where I was. At first, I assumed they were having a simple argument, nothing that concerned me. But being nosy, I stood there, eavesdropping. That's when I heard my name being mentioned. Curious, I continued to stand at there and listen to what they were saying, careful so as not to alert them to my presence. While arguing, I overheard my dad say, "I just want you to tell me the truth! I want you to be honest with me! Everyone is telling me you're cheating on me! Everybody is telling me you're using my American Express card to buy clothes for your man! Every year, you're going to Panama twice a year just to be with him! This is bullshit! I thought once we moved over here things would be different! When your mother told me that Nettie was not my child, I still accepted you..."

After hearing those words, my mind went blank for a moment. I couldn't hear anything else. I didn't want or need to hear anything else. That was undoubtedly the biggest shock of my life at that time. It was now confirmed. Everything Carmen said about me and others had been saying about me was true. That which I feared the most was a reality. I was not who I thought I was. Even more, dad wasn't who I thought he was. *What? Dad is not my real dad? Then who is he? Who am I? Who is my dad? How could mom hide this from me?*

I wanted to go to their bedroom door, knock on it, and confront them. I wanted to ask dad, "What did you just say? What do you mean grandma said I'm not your child?" Instead, I decided to go downstairs. I held it all in: the frustration, the anger; the questions bubbling in my soul, ready to burst out of me. I held it together long enough to get to the kitchen, which is where I let it all out. I burst into tears. I fell to my knees, crying, overwhelmed by emotion. It wasn't simply that I had just discovered I wasn't my dad's child, but I was emotional due to the fact that I had been lied to all my life by my mom, that secrets about my true identity had been withheld from me; I was emotional over the fact that the man I called father despised me due to those secrets and even wished me dead because of them. I was angry over the fact that my mom sat there and watched that man beat me mercilessly all over his bedroom and she refused to do or say anything; and now, I knew why. I knew why she didn't say anything, why she didn't stop the abuse that Walter, the man I called dad, inflicted on me: she knew that he knew I wasn't his child. She realized the pain Walter felt every time he looked at my face and into my eyes—I was a constant reminder of mom's infidelity, a reminder of the other man dad so furiously despised. It was eating him alive raising another man's child as his own, especially when lied to about the child's origins. There was always a question mark hanging over my head in Walter's eyes despite the fact that deep down within he'd already known I wasn't his.

I now knew why I felt like the ugly duckling in our family—it's because I was it. I was being treated like an outcast. That's why I was tasked with all of the cleaning, given the lowest and the worst jobs around the house. That's why my son was rejected by Walter. That's why he and my uncle wished me dead.

*

I was tired of it all, truly tired. Everything I had believed

CHAPTER 3: JUST LIKE CINDERELLA

about myself was a lie. I didn't know who I was anymore. My world had been turned upside down. I didn't know who to confide in, who to trust. I didn't feel accepted by my family, the guys I turned to seemed to only want one thing and nothing else, and the pain in my heart was too much to deal with, so I went into my mom's restroom and found a bottle of pills. My heart felt numb. Tears streamed down my eyes as I poured those pills into my hand. I just want this pain to end, I thought to myself as I lifted my hand to my mouth and swallowed a handful of pills.

    I digested the entire bottle of pills hoping I'd simply go to sleep and never wake up. But thank God those pills were water pills. I'd overdosed on water pills. They left me feeling woozy, a little lightheaded and tired, but nothing else. I called a friend of mine after that. He came and got me and took me over to his sister's house. She gave me some coffee and let me crash in her place for the night.

    I didn't go on a never-ending sleep like I'd planned. Quite the opposite; I woke up once more to what felt like a living nightmare. It was the same Brooklyn streets, the same smells and sounds; the same draggy, terrible feeling; the same headache brought on by overthinking; most importantly, the same problems at home I'd just attempted to escape from. The question was, should I try to end my life again, or should I learn to live with my situation? I suppose the scare of taking all of those pills shook me up because I didn't have the nerve to put myself through that situation again. It was only after my body rested and my mind settled for a moment from the cyclone of anxiety, confusion and anger that I started thinking about what I was about to leave behind. I'd forgotten for a brief moment about my two kids—my son and my daughter. I was in such pain that I was willing to inflict upon them the ultimate pain of losing a mother.

    Melissa's cries of not only snapped me back into the present, but they ushered me into a higher realm of purpose. How could I forget about them? With me gone, who would be there to protect them from the elements of this harsh world? Who would be there to guide them and wipe the tears from their little eyes? Who would be there to help spare them the pain I was experiencing due to lies and deep betrayal? They needed me, and I needed them. If there was no other reason for living, I'd adopted as my life's mission to be the type of mother to them that I felt I never had. I purposed in my heart that they wouldn't relive my curse, not as long as I can help it.

Chapter 4
AROUND THE BLOCK

Like I mentioned before, I was a sucker for guys with nice hair and who loved music. They had to be as big a music lover as me. And lo and behold, what better candidate to fit the description than a guy who was Trinidadian and was also a DJ (disc jockey). His name was Ricky. He had a head full of smooth, silky, curly hair and cute smile that made me melt. And yes, he was fine.

If there was ever a knight-in-shining-armor moment, this was it. I didn't have to act like a damsel in distress because I was one: still sinking emotionally in the bitter waters of strife and confusion. But hey, it didn't matter. I found a cute guy who could fill the empty spaces in my heart, one who would shower me with love and affection so that I could feel like a queen.

We were introduced by a casual acquaintance of ours. Ricky seemed nice. Again, he was handsome, he dressed nice, he had a good job and held similar interests as me. We immediately connected. There didn't seem to be anything out of the ordinary concerning him. He appeared to be a true gentleman.

But then again, there was one thing about him that was disturbing.

Ricky was well aware of my previous relationships. He knew Melissa's father, Neal, and that he lived across the street from me. So Ricky made it a point to always be around. He wanted to be near me at all times.

Now, in the beginning, I thought it was cute that Ricky wanted to be around me all the time, that he stayed in my face day-in and day-out; I suppose I viewed this as love or passion. To me, he certainly loved me. I was thinking he found me irresistible and just couldn't stand to be without me, and it felt good having someone treat me like that.

At first, Ricky and I were inseparable. Whenever he was performing somewhere, at a club or anywhere, I would go and support him. During his lunch breaks at his job, we would meet up and have lunch together. We hung out every weekend. He knew my favorite restaurant at the time was Red Lobster, and he would take me there all the time. Most of all, Ricky kept money in my pockets. Every week, he would give me money to buy the things I wanted and do the things I wanted to do.

Those first couple of months together felt like Heaven on earth. He was looking like a dream-come-true, a total dream guy—he had the looks, gave me everything I wanted, and was fiercely protective of me. Again, that fierceness seemed cute...in the beginning. But it started to take on a whole new meaning as time progressed. It started to feel a lot less flattering and much more like control. That's when

CHAPTER 4: AROUND THE BLOCK

the problem came.

Ricky kept me preoccupied pretty much all day, everyday. If he wasn't with me, he had me doing something for him. It didn't take long for me to catch on to what he was really up to: he was trying to keep me away from Neal. He didn't want me anywhere around Neal. The only problem was Neal was my daughter Melissa's father. And not only that, but I was very close to Neal's family. His parents were cool with me, and I was close to his sister, Jackie.

At first, I didn't really think much of the fact that Ricky held what I called impossible demands: he demanded that I not see my child's father; he demanded that I not be around my child's father's family; he demanded that I not interact with any of my baby-daddies and their families. Okay, dude, I can understand you wanting me all to yourself, but now you're getting out of hand. You're telling me who I can and cannot talk to like I didn't have a life before you. Again, I wanted to dismiss from my mind what was a clear red-flag, but it was getting harder to do so as Ricky's nice guy facade started to fade and I began to see his other side. And it was ugly.

DRAGGED

Melissa's aunt, Jackie, was moving to Coney Island, so I decided to help her pack. That day, I was at Neal's place helping with the move when suddenly the phone rang. It was Ricky. I chose not to answer the phone since I already knew what he was going to say. I didn't feel like arguing with him over my whereabouts. To a small degree, I did feel like I was obligated to communicate with him about my whereabouts since I was carrying his child, but we weren't engaged or married and I was a young adult woman capable of making my own decisions. Therefore, I ignored his call. I never anticipated how much that would affect him.

After a while, the phone rang again; this time, the number came from my house. When I answered the phone, it was my younger sister on the line. "Hello," I answered.

"Netti, Ricky's here," my sister responded. But before she could say anything else, Ricky snatched the phone out of her hand.

"Where you at?" Ricky asked forcefully.

"I'm at Coney Island helping Jackie move."

"Why didn't you answer the phone?"

"Because I knew you wouldn't want to hear I'm at Coney Island helping Jackie move," I sassed.

"I want you to meet me at such and such street," Ricky demanded in a serious tone.

"All right," I responded.

I drove to the street Ricky told me to meet him at, but he wasn't there. I figured he was playing games with me, trying to see if I would do what he told me to do. The entire situation just seemed petty to me. Why is he trippin' so hard? I thought.

After waiting for a while, it dawned on me that Ricky wasn't coming, so I put my gear into drive and began heading home. That's when my little sister called again, this time her tone was somber and worrisome. "Netti, Ricky just left and went outside. Right now, he's sitting in his car, waiting for you. He said, 'If your sister doesn't come home tonight, it's because I killed her.'"

CHAPTER 4: AROUND THE BLOCK

"What? He said that?" I asked, shocked.

"Yes, that's what he told me."

"All right," I said, mulling over those words in my head. I was wondering whether or not to take those words seriously. Never mind he said them. You'd think I would have been alarmed that Ricky had just threatened to kill me, which I was. But I figured he was just angry with me, and that he couldn't possibly be serious; that he couldn't possibly do what he threatened to do. He just running his mouth, trying to scare me, I thought to myself.

It didn't dawn on me that if Ricky threatened to kill me, whether or not he intended to make good on his promise didn't matter; what mattered the most was that he felt comfortable threatening my life, and had so little respect for me that he felt entitled to do so.

But I still didn't get it. I didn't take any of what he'd just said seriously. I simply went on my merry way.

When I arrived at the house, Ricky was there, sitting in his car, waiting on me. "Get in," he said sharply. Interestingly enough, he didn't seem angry. Tense, yes, but not irate. He seemed calm, probably a little too calm based on how he was talking earlier.

Once in his car, Ricky took off and began driving around the block. He was driving all over the place like he was looking for someone. He did this for some time.

Finally, it was getting pretty late. The whole time Ricky was driving, he didn't speak to me. He didn't say one word to me. He barely even looked at me. He seemed transfixed, lost in a daze, overcome with paranoid delusion, undoubtedly hoping to find someone. I figured he was trying to see if I was secretly meeting up with someone. Maybe he'd hoped to run into Neal on the street. I didn't know, but I suspected that much.

It was after midnight when Ricky decided to take me back home. Once there, without saying a word, he reached beneath the passenger seat and pulled out a pistol. I couldn't believe what I was seeing. It still hadn't dawned on me how serious he was at that moment. I thought he was playing, going to great lengths just to scare me. However, holding that gun in his hand, he looked me right in the eyes and said, "We're going back to Queens. You're not coming back here."

"What do you mean 'I'm not coming back here?'" I said laughingly. This can't be real, I thought to myself. But there was a look in his eyes that indicated I was in real danger. That look was one of menace, of ill-intent. He was dead serious.

"You're not coming back home, Netti," he sternly repeated. Right then, it hit me: this is a do or die situation. This guy is serious! This guy is crazy! I immediately jumped out of the car and ran towards the front door. He jumped out behind me and caught me before I could reach the door. "I said you're not going back home!" he yelled. He then began dragging me down the street by my hair. I'm kicking and screaming, trying to get loose, but couldn't. He dragged me towards a fire hydrant and then slammed my head into it. He repeatedly slammed my head into that fire hydrant until I nearly blacked out.

"Please, Ricky!" I screamed. His eyes were cold and calloused as if he had no soul while he continued to drag me by my hair up the street. The whole time he was dragging

CHAPTER 4: AROUND THE BLOCK

me, he was beating me—kicking me, slapping me, punching me in the face. He dragged and beat me all the way around the block, up one street and down another. This seemingly went on forever. I kept begging him, "Please, Ricky, stop!"

I remember shouting at him and telling him, "Ricky, stop! You know I'm pregnant! I'm pregnant with our child!" At the time, I was five months pregnant and it was starting to show. Three months after meeting, I had gotten pregnant with his baby.

I believe that was what saved my life that night: the reminder that I was pregnant. More importantly, it was the fact that I was carrying his child. You see, Ricky was happy over the fact that I was pregnant with his baby. He was ecstatic when I first broke the news to him. This was his second child—he'd had a child before we met. He actually looked forward to being a father, or perhaps, that what he made me think. Truthfully, he didn't appear too involved in his other child's life, so I had reason to doubt whether he would be a reliable father to our child.

When it was all said and done, I returned home looking a hot mess. My hair was tangled and looking wild. I was bleeding from my scalp from where he'd nearly pulled my hair out. My lips were busted and bleeding. My eyes swollen. My face was stinging. My sides hurt from being kicked and stomped. I was worried most of all that I'd lost the baby.

I remember going to the hospital to make sure the baby was okay. Thankfully, she was. I was done with Ricky on the other hand. I didn't want to see him, talk to him, or be anywhere around him ever again. I avoided him like a plague all the way up until the birth of our child.

FACE THE MUSIC

*

It was June 24, 1993, and I had just given birth to a beautiful little girl. I named her Fatima. Her little beady eyes staring up at me were like the eyes of an angel. My mom and my little brother was there to support me. Even Neal's brother, Andre, came by.

While I was in labor, I notified Ricky to tell him the baby was coming. That was my first time speaking to him since the incident on the street where he viciously attacked me. I figured that since the baby was his too, he at least deserved to witness the birth of our daughter. Ricky arrived late at the hospital. In those days, the nurses only allowed two visitors in a room at a time. So when Ricky showed up, it was just the two of us; everyone else had left. Ricky did witness Andre leaving the room though. And instead of entering the room and focusing on the baby, and instead of entering the room with flowers and an apology, the first thing he did upon entering the room was inquire as to why Neal's brother was there. Now, I'm in a recovery room with our baby in my arms. I'd just undergone a long, hard, physically taxing process of birthing a baby into this world. My body was weary, torn and worn out, and I barely had the strength to move. Now, Ricky was in my face, interrogating me about another man. "So, why was Andre there?" he asked.

"What do you mean 'Why was Andre here?'"

"So you think I'm stupid?" he retorted. WHAAP! I felt Ricky's hand go across my face. I was shocked that he would do that to me after I'd just given birth. Surely, he had to have some compassion in his heart towards me, after all

CHAPTER 4: AROUND THE BLOCK

I'd just gone through. Sadly, that wasn't the case. He started slapping me over and over again, beating right there in that hospital bed. Fortunate for him, my mom and little brother had already left and there was no one else in the room. If a nurse witnessed him hitting me, he would have been carried away in handcuffs to jail.

But it didn't matter that no one else saw him beating me in that hospital room; I knew what I was in for had I stayed in that relationship, and I didn't want that for myself. I no longer cared about the money, and I now saw Ricky's constant outpour of affection and attention for what it was: the smother antic of an insecure, jealous control freak. And I wasn't going to hang around any longer for what would have undoubtedly been the inevitable: death.

That's what I saw when I looked into his eyes while he was hitting me: rage and death.

FACE THE MUSIC

Chapter 5
SCREWED

*O*KAY, THAT'S IT! THIS IS THE LAST STRAW! RICKY PUT HIS HANDS *on me one too many times!* This time, my family witnessed it, and they weren't having it.

Ricky and I had just arrived home from the hospital. I didn't have a crib, a baby stroller, or anything for the baby. Ricky rudely tossed me some money and told me to go and get my own baby stroller—he was still fuming over the fact that Andre was at the hospital the day before. In a snarky manner, he told me to ask my little brother for help assembling the crib, and then he drove away, heading to work.

I managed to purchase a crib for the baby, and took it back home to assemble it. Andre happened to be at my house when I arrived. My brother and I began assembling the crib while Andre held the baby. He gently bounced the baby in his arms and talked to it, rocking her back and forth while making goo-goo sounds. Just then, Ricky entered into the house. I could see it on his face when he entered the house: he was annoyed that Andre was there. He simply looked at me and then stormed upstairs without saying a word, but I knew what that meant.

"Look, if I don't come downstairs in five-minutes, please come upstairs," I told Andre and my brother. I then proceeded upstairs to my bedroom where Ricky was waiting. When I entered the room, Ricky wasted no time slapping me around.

"I don't want my baby with that boy! I don't want my baby with that kid!" he yelled.

Walter happened to be home at the time. Both Ricky and all the commotion he caused was loud enough to get his attention. He then rushed to my bedroom, flung the door open and caught Ricky hovering over me preparing to strike me. "Get out!" he shouted at Ricky. Ricky gathered his stuff and left, and that was the last time he ever put his hands on me. That was also the last time we were ever together.

*

A year had passed and I moved on. I started dating another guy. Ricky would come by on the weekends to see our daughter, but I made sure we were never alone while together. Anytime he came over to see Fatima, I made sure there was someone else present with us: my mom, Walter, or my new boyfriend.

My new boyfriend was a musician. He played in a band. Now, I must admit that he was the total opposite of Ricky. With him, there wasn't the constant sense of being watched, there wasn't the feeling of being controlled; he didn't come across as possessive or insecure, always wanting to know my whereabouts and hovering over my shoulders

CHAPTER 5: SCREWED

every moment. He was cool and much more secure within himself.

He did everything for me. He was there when I needed him. He respected me. He was a good listener, had a rather mild and calm demeanor, and was incredibly supportive. He treated my kids like they were his own, seeing about them in the midnight hours so I could get some rest; fixing bottles and changing diapers for me. He even cooked and cleaned for us. He seemed like the perfect guy. But as I'd learned, whenever something seems too good to be true, it usually is. Unfortunately, that was the case here.

Ricky was too clingy; this guy was loose, so loose he had a hard time staying faithful. He was a serial cheater. He would try his best to cover his tracks, but like always, there are clues that get left behind in these instances: sudden smells, scents, odd behaviors and lies that lead to more lies among other things. After a while, I couldn't deal with it anymore.

Now, I shouldn't have to tell you that if you're going to cheat, it's important that you be discreet. In other words, keep your mouth shut. I suppose you can say that's the first lesson one learns in Cheating 101. But this guy didn't learn that lesson; he skipped that class. He was bold enough to go around bragging to his friends and others about his cheating. I guess he didn't think it would get back to me, which it did. I then confronted him and brought an end to that relationship. It was unfortunate because the two of us gave birth to a child. I had a daughter by him in 1998; her name was Ashley. She was my third daughter and fourth child. The two of us were together for eight-years. I really hoped we could have worked things out together, but he was too content with playing games and *chasing tail*.

WHERE'S MY MONEY

After a while, I'd gotten caught up in several criminal activities that eventually caught up with me. A single mother of six with five different baby-daddies, the chance of living a stellar life looked dim. What options were there for me? I wasn't college educated and I didn't have a particular skillset that was very useful in the workforce. I had a simple nine-to-five and nothing else going for myself. My luck with guys wasn't very good—either they were abusive or they were unfaithful. The only thing that brought a sense of adventure and promise of a better future for me was hustling.

I didn't sell crack or heroine like many in my neighborhood. My hustle was a little more subtle at the time: identity-theft. I was into credit card fraud. It all started one day after work. I used to work for a transportation service. We would gather customers' credit card information to place on file as a part of the job. I remember taking down one customer's credit card number and using it at a convenience store to buy a drink. It was so easy. I told the cashier I left my card by mistake and asked them if I could simply give them the card number, and they agreed. It was as simple as that. No ID check and no verification; simply lie and claim I lost my card and ask if I can provide the card number instead, then "bingo!"—I would get what I wanted. And it was a whole lot easier to do that over the phone. I began using different customer's credit card information to order expensive products from catalogues. I would order televi-

CHAPTER 5: SCREWED

sions, stereos, furniture, and all kinds of gadgets. I never had the items shipped to my address. I would have them shipped to certain drop off spots that couldn't be traced back to me.

During Christmas times and birthdays, I was considered a rockstar. I always came with the best gifts. I always had and provided the latest and greatest stuff. Few questioned how I was able to afford all of those gifts. But just in case anyone asked, I had my lie down-packed.

In the beginning, I was a lot more cautious with using people's credit card information. I was careful not to overdue it. However, as is typical, the temptation to go bigger and harder overcame me and I started using more and more credit cards from more and more customers. I then took it to another level and began applying for credit cards in customers' names. I figured I would do this for a little while and then stop, but like a drug, I couldn't resist the temptation to keep going.

I found a way to make plenty of money for myself through my activities. I began buying laptop computers using these credit cards and selling them to people on the streets. These were the newest and most sought after computers by Dell. They were selling like hot cakes. And not only that, but I began ordering the Nextel cellphones. These were really hot. Everyone wanted one of these phones. The demand for them on the streets pushed me to work that much harder to supply them. That meant more fraudulent credit cards ordered in more customers' names to order more phones.

In my mind, I fell for the classic lie that I could stop whenever I wanted to and leave the game before getting caught. I didn't think my sins would catch up with me. I was wrong. That is one law we can't avoid: we reap what we sow. Before long, stores began growing suspicious of my activities; they started requiring verification of identity in order to use a credit card to order from them. They added a security-questions layer, which made it difficult for me to order items using stolen credit card information. I couldn't answer the security questions. I mean, how was I to know what elementary school John graduated from, or the name of Jane's first pet? I began to get sloppy and guess at the answers, which raised a red flag with companies. And that's when things started to get hot.

In 2008, I packed up and moved to Virginia to stay with my sister for a little while, hoping things would die down back home. Again, I had raised too many red flags with credit card companies and retailers, and now they were on to me. While there, I figured I was safe. No one knew me. I felt like I was in the clear now, so I enrolled my kids in school and went on with my life. Then suddenly, I got a knock at my door; it was a distinctive knock, the kind that the police gives. *Boom! Boom! Boom!* "Open up! It's the police!"

Oh shit! I thought. *I'm screwed!* I had nowhere to run, nowhere to hide. My niece opened the door and I heard someone ask for me by name: "Antoinette Mitchel?" I came to the door.

"Yes, that's me."

"Please turn and put your hands behind your back. You have the right to remain silent. Anything you say can and will be used against you in a court of law. You have the

CHAPTER 5: SCREWED

right to an attorney . . ."

While the officer was handcuffing me, my mind was swirling with thoughts. I was thinking about my kids, what would happen to them. I was thinking about my family and if I would get to see them again. I had never been to jail before, so I thought about all of the stories and movies about jail I had heard and seen, trying to imagine what it would be like and what I might have to face. My nerves became unglued. I tried to hold it together, pretending to be unfazed like I was tough, but I was terrified.

In court, I was given an option of bail with the condition that I would turn myself in to the authorities in Pennsylvania where I was wanted for credit card fraud. I posted bail and then headed back to Pennsylvania where I had to stand before a judge and answer for my crimes. He ordered that I pay back the money I owed through fraud, which was around $25,000. This had to be paid within a few days or I would be sent to prison.

*

I had to get money quick to pay the courts, so I found another hustle, one that guaranteed fast money. I started trafficking drugs. All I had to do was transport the drugs from one place to the other, and when required, make money drops for drug dealers. This was a simple operation, an easy gig, or so I thought. However, nothing prepared me for the dangers of this game.

In order to appear inconspicuous, I purchased scrubs and dressed like a nurse; at other times, I'd dress like a doctor, wearing scrubs and the white coat. I even had a fake ID created for myself to further elude suspicion. I was transporting the cargo in a white van. On the long trips across state lines, I would get lonely and bored. By nature, I like to fellowship with people. I'm naturally talkative. Now, one cardinal rule in this industry was that mules (as they called us) had to travel alone whenever picking up or dropping off the merchandise. The dealers didn't play and couldn't take any chances. Violating the rules could cost you your life. I knew this, but I still broke the rules.

    One trip, I invited my nephew to come along. He made the trip with me, and I enjoyed his company. We talked and laughed while heading to our destination. Now, if you've ever been to New York City, then you're most likely familiar with the Brooklyn Bridge. On that bridge is a lane to the left that leads to a certain section of Brooklyn. Usually, that lane is very congested. My impatient self decided to drive in the moving lane and then cut in front of someone once I got close to where the lanes separated. I didn't feel like sitting and waiting in traffic. Once I cut in front of another car, the police saw me and pulled me over.

    I don't think my heart ever beat as fast as it did the moment I saw those blue and red lights in my rearview mirror. I had a ton of drugs in the back of the van. And not only that, but I didn't even have a driver's license. Yes, I had been driving for years without a driver's license. I never really prayed before then, but that time, I was praying inside. I was praying the policeman didn't check the van, for had he done so, that would have been the end of me. And being that I would have caused the dealers to loose a van-load full of drugs, I would have never been able to show my face in

CHAPTER 5: SCREWED

the hood again. I would have had a bullseye on my back.

"Excuse me ma'am, can I see your license and proof of insurance?" the officer requested.

"Uh, officer," I murmured, rumbling through my pockets and my purse, pretending to look for them. "Oh no, I left my license and insurance card back at the office by mistake. I'm so sorry."

"Well, ma'am, I can look you up by your name. What is your name?" I gave the officer one of my sister's names. He went and looked that name up and then returned to the van with a written ticket. I was so relieved that I had gotten off with only a ticket and a warning not to drive so recklessly. That was a close call for me and my nephew.

*

Now you would think after my close call with the police I would have learned, but I didn't. I continued to traffic drugs and break the rules while doing it. This time, I invited a dude I'd met to go along with me on a drug run. My assignment was to drop off a bag of money to a dealer. No one was supposed to be with me, especially considering I had over $40,000 on me. However, I didn't follow instructions because I didn't feel like making such a long trip by myself.

Knowing the risk of being seen with someone else in the van, I instructed the guy I was with to hide in the back while I received the money from my pickup spot. Once I got the money, I simply tossed the bag of money in the back of the van and drove off, heading to my drop-off spot where I had to deliver the money. The guy I had to drop the money off to was a well known dealer known as "C". He had a serious reputation and would hurt you if you messed with his money or merchandise.

While heading to where C was, I was running my mouth, talking to the guy in the back of the van riding along with me. I didn't think he would rummage through the bag filled with money, but he did. He was going through that bag and stuffing the money into his pockets. Before I pulled up to where C was, I told the guy to get out of the van so he wouldn't be discovered. Again, I forgot I had placed the money back there with him. So when he got out, he left with most of the money. How he managed to stuff nearly forty-thousand dollars in his pockets, I don't know, but he did.

After letting the guy out of the van, I drove to where C was. C came out and looked for the money, but all he found was an empty bag. He asked me where his money was. I was shocked to find out it was gone. Right then, it dawned on me who had it: the guy who was riding with me. He stole it. But I couldn't tell C since I wasn't supposed to have anyone with me to begin with. I knew that if I'd confessed that the money was stolen by someone I took with me, I would have been in even more trouble. So I simply told C I didn't know what happened to the money.

You can imagine how I looked at that moment. Over forty-thousand dollars was gone, and I was the last person with it in my possession. C perceived me as a thief. What else was he to think? He then threatened that I had better return his money, or else. And I didn't have long to get him his money either. I believe the only reason he didn't kill me on the spot was because we grew up together. But I was in a serious jam. I owed over $25,000 to the courts, and now

CHAPTER 5: SCREWED

I owed over $40,000 to one of the biggest drug dealers in town. I was screwed.

FACE THE MUSIC

Chapter 6
LOST AND FOUND

"**Ms. Mitchel, do you have the money** I ordered you to pay back the court?"

"No, sir, your honor, I don't have all of the money—I only have some of it."

"That's not what I instructed you to bring. You were ordered to pay the whole amount before our next court date."

"I know, your honor, but I have half of it. Can I just pay half and then pay the rest later? I promise I'll get the full amount over to you."

"Ms. Mitchell, I'll be honest with you, I'm glad you didn't show up to court today with the full amount, because if you did, I'd be curious as to where you got the money from. So I am sentencing you to six-months in the Lehigh County Jail...."

There I was, being sentenced to six to twenty-three months in prison. But to be honest, that was better than remaining on the streets and facing C, which was undoubtedly a death sentence. I can do six months. I can handle this. All I have to do is stay out of trouble, don't get caught up into mess and drama, keep my head straight and serve my time. I'll be out in no time.

PRISON

I walked through the steel doors of Lehigh County Prison in March of 2009. That was a new experience, one I never plan to relive. While in prison, there was a constant sense of walking on eggshells. To be honest, I didn't see a lot of crazy stuff. There weren't a lot of fights or assaults like you would see in the movies, but there was always a heavily combustable tension in the air that kept everyone on edge. Whether it was a fear of the correctional officers or an inmate, you knew to tread softly and carefully. I mean, I wasn't sharing space with a group of beauty pageant contestants. Some of those girls were mean, hardened criminals. Some were in there for murder, for committing some of the craziest and most insane acts. Some of them were dealing with mental health issues. This wasn't Disney World.

I basically stayed to myself while there. I didn't interact too much with others. The only thing I did was read the Bible. Before then, I had never even picked up a Bible. I never cared to. But now, as they say, God got my attention. Call it jailhouse religion. Call it what you want to. It doesn't matter. The truth is, when you have nowhere else to turn and no one to turn to, when you're surrounded by people who are losing their minds and doing some of the craziest things to themselves and to others; when fear, anxiety and depression consumes you and nearly drives you into a pit

CHAPTER 6: LOST AND FOUND

of insanity, what better time to reassess your life and your values and think about what is really important in life? You have very few distractions in jail. You can no longer smoke and drink away your problems. You can't run and hide from life while there. What better time to focus on God. Or better yet, what better time for God to call your name.

ON THIN I.C.E.

I had taken much for granted in my life at that time. I mean, the fact that I was still alive was by the grace of God; I shouldn't have been breathing. But I was just living wild and recklessly, not caring about the consequences of my actions—and best believe, they carried some serious consequences as I was about to discover.

I forgot I that I was still considered an immigrant to America. I had a green card that allowed me to stay here, but that was contingent upon me following certain rules. One of the main conditions for me remaining in America was that I couldn't get locked up for any crime other than a small misdemeanor or a traffic violation. Any crime that carried a prison sentence of six-months and higher was grounds for an automatic deportation. I had been sentenced to six to twenty-three months with a mandatory six-month prison term and the rest of my time to be served out on probation.

I'd broken the cardinal sin of immigration: I got myself in serous trouble with the law, and now, I was about to pay for it. Out of the blue, I had received a sudden visit from a woman who was from the Immigration and Customs Enforcement (ICE). She had no personality. She came and asked me a bunch of questions and asked me if I had my green card, all of which I'd answered to the best of my ability. After that, she explained to me that I would be deported immediately after my prison sentence was up. I asked her why they were deporting me, and she answered that I violated the conditions of my immigration status by getting locked up for my criminal behavior and activities. I tried to explain to her that I was unaware of the conditions of my staying here because I came to America as a little girl, but she didn't care. She finished up her questioning, reiterated to me what was going to happen next, and then exited the room.

Before that, I had never heard of ICE. I didn't know that any such organization existed. But now, I knew.

After the woman left, I was just sitting in my chair, trying to figure out what to do. My mind was swirling with a ton of thoughts, worries and concerns. Deportation meant I was going to be sent away from my home—I considered America as my home because that's where I had grown up—forever. I would never be allowed to return to this country. I mean, I could do prison time; that didn't worry me so much because after that was done, I would be allowed to go back home. But now, I was being threatened with the possibility that I would never be allowed to return home. Now I was scared. I began to think about all of the people I would never see again and all of the things I would miss. I thought about my children and my family. I thought about my neighborhood and the opportunities I had in this country. It dawned on me that I was about to lose a lot, more than I could handle losing.

After the visit from ICE, I immediately called my

CHAPTER 6: LOST AND FOUND

son and told him what happened. "But mom, you've been here all these years, your whole life. They can't just deport you just like that," my son replied, shocked.

"Look, that lady didn't care. She was serious: they plan to deport me. I just have to fight this."

My son promised to find an immigration lawyer for me. All I could do was hope and pray at that point. It's not like my family had a bunch of money lying around to go towards my legal defense anyway. I didn't know what to do or where to turn.

A LIGHT IN THE DARKNESS

When I first arrived at Lehigh County Prison, I was placed in a medical holding cell as was and is customary whenever one is first locked up. Afterwards, I was sent into the general population where I met another inmate. The two of us started talking while there. She was telling me about prison and giving me a few survival tips. And while she was talking, a guard entered the room and asked if either one of us wanted to go to church. There was a prison ministry group that would visit the prison on a weekly basis. The girl answered no; and because she turned down the offer to go, so did I. Once the guard left, she turned back towards me and began talking against those church services. She accused the ladies who attended them as "playing games" and going just to escape. Several hours later, she was released from prison.

The following day, the guards moved me to another room. While there, I met another girl. Her name was Kelly. She was in the same boat as me, facing deportation. We began talking, and she started telling me about how amazing the church services were and encouraging me to attend. I was still thinking about what the other girl said about the church services, so I chose not to go.

That girl would attend every church service and then come back brag and to me about what I missed. It was the excitement in her voice that won me over and made me want to go. I could tell she was genuinely excited about what she was experiencing; and not only that, but she would return from those services with such a peace and sense of joy that it baffled me. If anything, I was more curious about what was going on at those services than anything, and felt the need to see for myself what was happening. So one day, I decided to go. That was the day my life changed.

I remember sitting in that room, watching everyone and everything. Mind you, this was my first time going to church, so I was already nervous just being there. I didn't know what to expect. At first, there was a group of people at the front of the room singing worship songs to God. They sounded good, but I didn't know any of the songs. I just sat and observed. As those people (the ministry group) were singing at the front of the room, I noticed several of the other inmates standing and singing along with them; some of them had their hands lifted, their eyes closed, and they sung as if they didn't have a care in the world. Some of them were crying. That made me feel weird at first.

Suddenly, during the service, a woman began ministering. She was speaking in Spanish, but she had a translator translating her words into English where I could understand. Everything was going fine until that woman came over to me and singled me out. She pointed at me and asked

CHAPTER 6: LOST AND FOUND

me to approach the front of the room. At first, I was looking around, thinking she was speaking to someone sitting behind me. But then I realized she was speaking to me. My blood was rushing. My mind was filled with all kind of thoughts. *Is she going to embarrass me? Humiliate me? Ask me to do something silly? Oh my God, is she going to ask me to sing? What does this lady want with me? And why me? Why is she calling on me out of all people?* I got up out of my chair and slowly and nervously made my way to the front, to the stage where the minister was. While there, she asked me if that was my first time at one of their services. I said yes. First she thanked me for coming, and then she placed her hand on my chest and started speaking what sounded to me like gibberish. Suddenly, she stopped and looked up at me and said, "I have a message for you: You have to forgive." I knew exactly what she was referring to. She didn't even have to go into detail.

Those words pierced me like an arrow. I began to feel a flood of emotion rising inside of me. At first, I got angry at Kelly for inviting me there. I thought she told that minister all of my personal business, thereby causing her to put me on the spot. But I realized Kelly had nothing to do with this. And plus, Kelly never knew about my relationship with my mother. Whatever was happening, it was supernatural. I had never experienced anything like that before.

My tears began to flow. Up until then, I had made it my mission to conceal my tears and hide my emotions. I didn't want anyone to see me cry—I had to maintain a tough exterior. But now, I was standing in front of a room full of people and crying. As the lady continued to place her hand gently on my chest, I felt a warm sensation come all over me; it was like a gentle and loving presence gently overshadowing me. That made me feel even more vulnerable, as if a wall in my heart was being demolished. After that, she was through. That was all she said to me. I went back to me seat and just sat there, thinking about what was said and trying to make sense of what just happened.

How did she know? I asked myself. No one in that prison knew I was full of anger and unforgiveness towards my mother. That anger and hatred ran deeper than any other emotion I felt, even deeper than the fear of being deported; it imprisoned my soul. Sure, I was doing time in a physical prison, but the real prison I was locked up in was the one in my heart and mind. I could feel the cold steel of hatred and bitterness. My mind was held captive by confusion and fear. When I was outside of Lehigh Prison's walls, I was miserable. I'd spent so much of my life running from my pain and distracting myself from my own memories, doing whatever I could to avoid thinking about the unresolved issues in my life. But now, I was in a place where I couldn't run. I just had to stay there and face what I had tried so hard to ignore.

*

I went back to my bed still shaken up from that church service. Kelly was right: that was life-changing. I kind of felt like my head was in a fog. And although I couldn't wrap my head around what had just happened, that experience birthed something within me: a desire to want to know God. If He sent that lady to prison just to deliver a message to me, I wanted to know who He was. Furthermore, I wanted to

CHAPTER 6: LOST AND FOUND

ask Him a few questions like, *Where were you all of this time in my life? Why didn't you come and help me when I was being abused as a child? Why did you hide yourself from me for so long? What do you want with me?*

The more I thought about everything, the more I started to question myself. I began to feel bad about myself. I felt bad because for the first time in my life I discovered God truly exists and that He actually cared about me. This troubled me because I had never cared about Him. I had never taken the time to talk to Him or acknowledge Him. The only god I worshipped at that time was self. I was only focused on me and what I wanted. And now I felt guilty for ignoring Him all this time. I wondered how He viewed me. Did He view me as a disappointment? I had been told all my life that's what I was. I had been called worthless and good for nothing, talked down to and overlooked, and made to feel like a failure in every way. And I knew that regarding the matter of righteousness and holiness, I definitely didn't add up. I did everything a righteous God would frown upon, and now, that same God was calling me. I didn't feel worthy enough to answer the call. I didn't feel good enough to be or do whatever He was calling me to be or do.

The good thing is I kept reading my Bible. Despite how I felt, I kept doing that. In fact, my hunger to read the Bible intensified after that worship experience. Maybe I didn't have it all together, but I at least developed an interest in somebody other than myself—at least I was curious about God and why He created me. I would have never developed such and interest had I not been where I was and experienced what I did.

FACE THE MUSIC

Chapter 7
STRANGE VISITORS

DAY AFTER DAY, NIGHT AFTER NIGHT, I WOULD LIE IN my bed and read the Bible. I didn't want to read any other book. It was now an obsession of mine. It amazed me how much I had overlooked such an incredible gem in my life. In the projects, it was normal, almost customary, to see a Bible sitting on someone's mantlepiece or table; they would usually there for decoration purposes. Now, I was actually reading one, and the things I was learning from it were exciting to me.

I started in the Book of Genesis, the book of beginnings. Of course, where else would I start? I wanted to know how it all started between God and man. I wanted to know who God was and why He was so interested in me as a person. Every week, I attended the church services and basked in the worship experience. I went from being critical of church to loving it. I never imagined that I would be the one standing on my feet during worship with my hands lifted and tears streamed down my cheeks while singing praises to

God. But there I was.

I would listen intently to the messages the minister would give and then go back to my bed and study the Bible further. I never missed a day of studying the Bible. I began listening to Bible teachings from other ministers such as Joyce Meyers and others. I felt like a kid who had discovered an entirely new world I didn't know existed, one that was right beneath my nose the whole time.

Joyce Meyers testimony resonated with me. It was shocking to say the least. The things she described going through shook me to the core. But what was impressive to me was the fact that she, like Kelly, had this incredible joy, love and resolve even in the face of amazing adversity. If there was one thing I wanted, one thing I longed for more than anything else in this world, it was to be able to genuinely smile. I wanted to be free in my heart and mind, not just physically. In fact, I preferred mental and emotional freedom over physical freedom; at least then, I would be able to live with myself, I would be able to sleep fully at night and arise with peace; I would finally enjoy living, even look forward to the next day. Suicidal thoughts replaced the sunshine in my mind. Hatred and self-loathing were like dark clouds hovering over my head, causing me to languish in a state of perpetual dread. I dreaded getting up in the morning. I hated myself. I often wondered and even asked myself how many more days I had left. I would have images in my head of me dead, either the victim of suicide or a violent homicide. Depression put me in a desperate place. I longed to be free. Drugs couldn't do it. Alcohol couldn't either. Sex couldn't free me. All of these things offered a temporary

CHAPTER 7: STRANGE VISITORS

buzz that quickly went away and left me feeling just as empty, if not emptier, than before. God had to rescue me—I was at the end of my rope.

My new preoccupation was a breath of fresh wind; it breathed new life into me. It was different from everything else I had tried. Pursuing God was better than pursuing temporary relief and momentary happiness. Even though I wasn't entirely free from the grip of depression and fear, I was on a journey that gave me strength and hope in the midst of what I was battling. Furthermore, I sensed for the first time ever that I was not alone, that I had help in this fight.

*

I had read the Bible multiple times from cover to cover while there at Lehigh. I attended the church services regularly and kept myself preoccupied with positive things. One of my favorite characters in the Bible was King David. His life seemed to mirror mine. I could study him all day long. He fascinated me because of all of the things he had to endure and overcome to become the king of Israel. Here was this kid who possessed awesome potential and a fierce confidence, but he was despised by his own father. Sounded familiar. As a child, he was rejected by his family and never quite felt like he belonged. Truthfully, he stood out like a sore thumb from his siblings. He was considered the black sheep of the family and assigned the task of overseeing the family's sheep on the backside of the desert where the most dangerous animals were known to roam. He was overlooked and often forgotten about; and yet, God chose him. It didn't matter that David's brothers were better groomed for the position of king; God picked this scrawny little kid to be the next king of Israel. Why? Because his heart was in the right place. What that story said to me was some people might not see you and value you, but it doesn't matter what people say or do; God sees you and He values you. He has placed within you greatness, and your worth is not determined by other's opinions of you.

Furthermore, as David is the same person who wrote Psalms 27:10, which says, "Even if my father and mother abandon me, the LORD will hold me close" (NLT).

The first lesson God had to teach me was that my worth as a person wasn't determined by my mom or Walter; it was determined by Him. I'm sure that's a lesson all of us must learn to be honest. The source of our identities is God, not our parents. This was further evidenced in Scriptures such as Psalm 139:13-14 and Jeremiah 1:5, which says,

> "You made all the delicate, inner parts of my body and knit me together in my mother's womb. Thank you for making me so wonderfully complex! Your workmanship is marvelous—how well I know it." (NLT)

> "I knew you before I formed you in your mother's womb. Before you were born I set you apart and appointed you as my prophet to the nations." (NLT)

That was exciting to discover! I'm a piece of work—or put another way, I'm God's marvelous workmanship! That's a to-

CHAPTER 7: STRANGE VISITORS

tally different message from what I had received from my mother and from Walter. Walter told me I was worthless and that I was better off dead, and my uncle said the same. My mom may not have uttered those exact words to me, but her actions spoke louder than words. She lied to me about my past, about who my father was, sat quietly and watched as Walter threw me around his room and beat me from one end of it to another. It seemed to me that she was more interested in keeping a man than protecting her daughter. Even more, she acted as if it was a small thing that I had been molested by another family member. All she wanted was to keep the peace by making me suppress my emotions.

Now, I was hearing a different message about myself. God was telling me I mattered. He was informing me I deserved to exist. And not only that, but He was letting me know that there was more inside of me that I could have imagined, that I had greatness stored up on the inside of me just waiting to be unleashed. That I was gifted and endowed with purpose. My challenge was believing all of this.

I kept reading the Bible. I wanted to know more about God. I became hungry for Him. I didn't know anything about religion. If you asked me anything about church denominations, I couldn't answer you because I wasn't interested in that stuff; I was only interested in God.

STRANGE VISITORS

My six months at Lehigh County Prison were up. Immigration showed up and transferred me to York County Prison in Pennsylvania where they held both regular inmates and immigrants. Here, inmates were held in prison cells. I shared cells with a girl named Anne. Both of us were transferred from Lehigh at the same time. The authorities wanted us to stay together because Anne was on suicide watch. She had lost her husband while locked up. He was killed in a car accident after visiting her. It had to be devastating for her not being able to lay his body to rest and not being able to console her children. She was inconsolable at times.

Many nights, Anne would burst into tears and I would do my best to comfort her. But I often struggled to find the words to say. I could only imagine how she must have felt and what she was going through. My heart broke for her. All I could do was become a listening ear.

Our first week at York County Prison, me and Anne were sitting on the bottom bonk; she was sobbing uncontrollably. I was trying to comfort her the best I could, but I had grown too tired to stay awake and decided to go back down to my bonk and get some rest. I went to sleep to the sound of Anne crying. A few hours later, I was awakened by someone calling my name. I realized it wasn't Anne because she was sound asleep, and that voice didn't resemble *hers*. *The voice was coming from the area by our cell door. Maybe it's a correctional officer. But why would they call my name like that? And I didn't hear any keys.* I laid there nervously, covers over my head, staring in the direction of the door. I soon started to drift off to sleep again; my eyelids overcome by the heaviness of slumber. Then suddenly, I heard my name being called again: "Antoinette."

Whoever it was calling my name did so in a strange manner: their voice wasn't authoritative like one of the correctional officers; it was gentle, but carried with it a depth

CHAPTER 7: STRANGE VISITORS

that penetrated my innermost being. I pulled the covers down and looked in the direction of the door, and that's when I saw it: there were two luminous beings standing by the door. It was strange because I couldn't see their faces. It was as if their faces were as black as night, like they were invisible. I couldn't tell if they were male or female. They were wearing white robes. The light that emanated from their bodies didn't fill the entire cell like one would expect; it mainly stayed around them like an aura. Their height and size were normal although they were anything but normal. Initially, I was clueless as to who or what these beings were. I didn't know if they were aliens, ghosts, demons, or what. I kind of ruled out the idea of them being aliens because they didn't look like little green men; they looked human. But other than that, I didn't know. Or maybe a part of me just didn't want to admit what they were.

Prior to this, I had only read about angels in the Bible. I had heard of them, but I never took the subject too seriously. I kind of dismissed them as simply the stuff of legend or fantasy. And now, I was looking at them. It was surreal, like something out of a dream.

Thank God for the Bible; it confirmed what I had experienced. I remember coming across a biblical passage about a young man named Samuel. He was just a child at the time, and was living with the High Priest of Israel, Eli. One night, Samuel heard a voice calling his name. He arose thinking it was Eli although it wasn't. Two more times that voice called out to him. And in both instances, he arose, thinking it was Eli calling him. But Eli, being older, wiser and perceptive, realized what was really going on, he realized that it was God calling out to Samuel. He then told Samuel to answer and say, "Yes, Lord, here am I" the next time he heard that voice call his name. Thankfully, Samuel had a coach who knew how to respond to that situation, but I didn't have a coach. This was all new to me. I didn't know what to say or what to do. So I put my covers back over my head and balled up in the fetal position like a baby, shivering with fear and praying to God to make those beings go away. I was terrified out of my mind, just hoping they wouldn't attack me and carry me off somewhere.

I was frozen with fear, too afraid to scream or do anything. I so desperately wanted to awaken Anne so that she could see what I was looking at. I didn't know if that would help any or even if she would be able to see the entities. I didn't know what to do, so I closed my eyes and tried to pretend I was simply having a bad dream. When I reopened my eyes, the beings were gone. They'd simply vanished.

I could hardly sleep after that. I basically stayed awake the whole night, thinking they might return. And I hardly slept the following night. Throughout the day, I was looking over my shoulder the whole time, and I didn't want to be alone at any time. That was the last time I saw them though. They never did return. And I never heard a mysterious voice call my name at night or experienced anything like that again. But that whole experience was an eye-opener; it let me know there are things in this world and universe we cannot fully explain; that there are beings who're all around us that we cannot see. That experience let me know the spirit world is real.

Chapter 8
CRAZINESS

BEFORE I WAS VISITED BY THE TWO ANGELS, I HAD another strange encounter, but this one was with a human: it was a girl I had met during my first week at the new prison. Her name was Keisha. That morning, we were sitting at the breakfast table together. Now, I didn't know her and she didn't know me. We had never met before. But suddenly, she decided to introduce herself. "Hello, my name is Keisha," she said.

"I'm Antoinette."

"Nice to meet you, Antoinette." She then took a slight pause as if contemplating what to say next or how to say what she really wanted to say, and then she continued, "I don't want you to think I'm crazy or anything, but I see that you have a long fight ahead of you. Let me explain. I'm a prophetess. I see you signing a lot of papers, but you're going to win this. You're going to be signing a lot of papers though, and it's going to take you a while."

A prophetess—that was the first time I'd ever met

anyone that called him or herself that. From reading the Bible, I had become familiar with the term though; but again, I didn't think much of it. But when she announced herself as that, I was amazed. Here this girl was, an inmate just like me, sitting behind bars for some crime, and yet, she wore a title I thought only belonged to the holiest of men, the purest of souls. Sure, never mind the fact that the Bible says no one is perfect and that we all sin and fall short of the glory of God; I simply hadn't grasped fully the fact that God can use anyone anywhere and at any time.

Of course, part of me was curious as to why this girl was locked up with me, but I knew better than to pry into her personal life. I just sat back and listened and took in what she was saying. I didn't tell her my status: that I was facing deportation. She had no way of knowing what I was up against. For all she knew, I could have been just another American citizen locked up for a crime, facing time. Again, she didn't know me. But God did. And I took that as a sign that He was looking after me and that things were going to work in my favor. I needed that. For months, I had wondered about my case, about my chances, thinking about how torturous it would be to be without my family and not be in my kids' lives, to not see my old neighborhood and visit my childhood friends, to not be able to visit the place I'd called home for nearly forty years of my life. And now, there was a glimmer of hope in my eyes. Keisha gave me hope.

I suppose that's what faith is, or at least, what it is designed to do: provide hope to the hopeless. And I was surely one of them. So many girls I was locked up with were in that state of mind. They had given up all hope of ever returning

CHAPTER 8: CRAZINESS

home. Many of them who were facing deportation acted and behaved like they didn't stand a chance of remaining in the United States of America. But I felt like the lucky one. I had been singled out by a minister just several months prior and given hope as it pertained to my personal life—informed that God sees me and that He wants to heal my heart from the pain of my childhood. That was comforting because I thought no one saw me crying in the midnight hours as a little girl. I thought no one cared about my pain. I thought I'd done a good enough job of concealing the wounds that were festering in my soul. Just smile and pretend they're not there. Just run and play as if my heart wasn't broken. Just continue on with life as usual as if mine hadn't gotten trapped in the past. But God saw me crying and had a plan to turn my tears into diamonds.

And now, I was being injected with the hope of a brighter tomorrow and told that I was going to "win". The state, no matter how big, bad and strong it was, wasn't going to get what it wanted: to deport me. I mean, I thought about that. *What could little ole' me do against the all powerful government of the United States of America? What fight could I put up?* I couldn't even afford an attorney to represent my case. So what could I have done. But the revelation of one who is bigger than man and any government fighting on my side was all I needed. I hung my heart on those words and found a new strength. I almost felt giddy, like I wanted to break down and cry happy tears. I burden had lifted from my shoulders, the pressure on my chest had eased, the stress in my mind began to dissipate, and my trial hadn't even gotten started yet. But I had an assurance. I now had something far greater than a lawyer and money; I had faith: a divine assurance that God had already worked things out for me and that I would be free to go home when it was all said and done. Now I just had to wait.

THE DREAM

As if it wasn't enough that I'd just received one of the greatest confirmations in my life from a girl I had never met, I could feel the strings of my heart being pulled once again by the Big Man upstairs. This time, I wasn't visited by an angel or approached by a human agent of the unseen world; I had an unusual dream.

In the dream, I saw an aunt of mine who died. She looked healthy and strong, just the way I liked to remember her. She had called my mom and enthusiastically told her that I beat my case and that I was coming home. I could see them jumping for joy while celebrating my victory. My mom started shouting, "Netti won! She beat the case! She's coming home!"

Suddenly, I woke up.

The dream felt so real to me; it was like I was literally there. It didn't seem like a regular dream; this one was different. Again, I took it as a sign that things were going to work out for my good and lean in my favor.

Prior to that, I had never experienced what I would call supernatural dreams and visions from God or any other source for that matter. Again, the supernatural was just an afterthought to me. I didn't prepare for it, look for it, seek after it, or even pray for it. I had given up on any supernatural intervention a long time ago, when I was a child praying

CHAPTER 8: CRAZINESS

for my nightmare to end. Nothing happened then and I suspected that nothing would ever happen. But all of this began happening once I started reading the Bible and turning my attention towards God. At first, it was done in curiosity. But after that visit from the minister that day, I developed a thirst for the God of the Bible. And now, it was as if one supernatural occurrence after another was taking place in my life. During one of the worst seasons of my life, I was undergoing the greatest experiences. While in the worst place, I was having the time of my life. Odd! I know. But that's how it happened. I'd read about God giving men supernatural dreams in the Bible: Joseph, the great savior of Egypt who was thrown into a pit and then sold into slavery before languishing in a prison for several years all because God gave him a dream that he was going to rule over his brothers; King Nebuchadnezzar who was given a dream about the coming world empires that would rule after him, which was interpreted by the prophet Daniel; even the Apostle Peter who was visited by God in a dream and shown where his next ministry assignment was. So God uses dreams, and I knew in my heart of hearts that this was a dream from Him.

*

The question is, *Why?* Why was all of this so important: the prophecies, the visitation, and the dream? I was getting a crash course in faith and didn't know it. This would mark the beginning of my true life, a life of faith, a journey of discovery when it comes to my purpose. As strange as it might sound to some, God had to put me in the right place to teach me who He was and to teach me what faith was. *Why* couldn't I just learn it in a church? Why couldn't I discover all of this while sitting in a cozy Sunday School class? In fact, why was I born into a family with such problems, one that didn't focus on God and go to church? How come God didn't let me come up in a God-fearing, church-going, devoutly religious home where angels and demons, Heaven and Hell, righteousness and wickedness, sin and salvation were routinely discussed? I came up like a heathen, having hardly any understanding of God at all. There was only one conclusion I could reach: there was a purpose for me being here. I needed to learn all of this because it serves my purpose. Furthermore, I needed to see both sides of the coin: the good and the bad. I had to experience what it was like to be wounded so I could value and appreciate what it feels like to be healed.

I know I wouldn't have taken God seriously before I encountered my struggle. It took a prison cell to set me free. Other than that, I would still be in bondage to this day, if not dead. While in York County Prison, I devoted myself to the study of the Bible. I even took Bible classes while there. I won an award for studying the Bible and was awarded a special Bible. There was an organization that would administer tests to the students in the Bible Study course. I passed all of those exams with flying colors. None of that would have interested me had I not found myself in the place I was in. God had to spark a fire inside of me that would transform me from the inside out, and I'm grateful that He did it that way.

Not only was this the reason for the divine confirmations; but I needed them because of the long road ahead of me. There would be nights when I would ask "God, where

CHAPTER 8: CRAZINESS

are you?" It would be during those times when I would have to pull on everything that was inside of me to keep from . . .

LOSING IT

A group stopped by the prison and presented those of us without legal representation with the opportunity to receive an attorney pro bono. They emphasized that there was no guarantee that we would get one pro bono, but if we filled out and submitted the paperwork to sign up for their program, there was a chance. I was like, Hey, what do I have to lose? I don't have any money and my family can't afford a lawyer, so why not? If I get selected, then good; if not, then oh well. I submitted my paperwork and then waited patiently to hear back from them.

Time had passed and before I knew it, I was being transferred to another prison, Cambria County Prison—I'd spent six months at York County Prison. Upon entering Cambria, I immediately requested to make a phone call. I wanted to call home and wish my baby girl a happy birthday. My kids were still young and didn't know what was going on with me. They had no idea where I was, which was what I wanted. I would call and speak with them from time to time just to let them know I was safe and that I would see them soon.

When I called, my sister answered the phone. We spoke for a second and then she passed the phone to my daughter. "Hi, baby girl, I just wanted to wish you happy birthday!"

"Hi, mommy, where are you? We're here, waiting for you to come and watch a movie with us." I don't know how

FACE THE MUSIC

I held it together, but I did in that moment. When she said those words to me, my knees grew weak and I felt as if I had just been punched in the gut. It felt like I had just gotten the wind knocked out of me. I wanted to bust out into tears at that moment, but I couldn't. So I just told her I loved her and promised that I would see her soon and then got off of the phone.

When I reached my bed, I fell apart. That was one of the few times that I broke down in tears in front of people. I couldn't hold it in. I felt so horrible that I couldn't be there for my kids, that I couldn't hug and kiss my baby girl on her birthday. It dawned on my just how precious those little moments we tend to take for granted are. Just to sit barefooted in front of a television and watch a princess movie with my little girl was more valuable than all the money in the world at that moment. Just to feel her warmth, see her smile, hear her giggle, and feel her little hands touching me was my deepest desire. It started to feel like hell being in that place. Those prison walls were now beginning to feel like prison walls—they were the things holding me back from experiencing my child's gentle embrace; they were the barriers trapping me in a state of separation from those I loved. I didn't care about all of the subtle nuances that make prison what it is: the bland colored walls; the small cells that feel like they're closing in on you after a while, causing you to feel claustrophobic; the correctional officers who talk to you like you're a dog; the less than stellar food; the confinement, strict schedule, monotonous routines that make you feel like a robot, and the humiliating things such as having to shower in front of everyone or be subject to lockdowns and degrad-

CHAPTER 8: CRAZINESS

ing searches. I could deal with those things. I could adjust to them. But what I found unbearable was thinking about the lost time between me and my kids, how they were growing up and reaching milestones in their lives without me. I began to fear if I would ever get out of that place and get back to them, or if I would only have to hear about their proms and weddings from a third party. I was terrified of a future without them in my life, a future where I was either locked up in a strange place of forever locked out of a familiar one.

While sobbing, I put my headsets on and tried to drown out my sorrow by listening to music on my walkman. It just so happened that there was a song on by a Christian artist named Plumb; the song was entitled *Beautiful History*. It went:

> *I am here.*
> *I'm holding you.*
> *You'll make it through this.*
> *I am here.*
> *I am here.*

It was as if God was singing them to my spirit. They soothed the pain in my heart and quieted my mind. All I wanted to do was marinate in that voice and play those words over and over again in my mind. I didn't want to think about anything else, just visualize and imagine in that moment the arms of God wrapping around me like a warm blanket. I just laid there in my bed and wrapped my arms around myself as if they were the arms of God. I needed to feel an embrace. I needed to not feel so alone. Yes, in prison, I was surrounded by people, and several of them were now my friends, but none of them were my family. And plus, regarding the inmates, there was no guarantee that any one of them would be around for long. We were always being transferred; some of us deported. So, no, there wasn't a sense of stability. All of this made me feel isolated and alone. And now, I was beginning to feel desperate.

*

What's taking these people so long? I wondered. I was simply waiting and waiting, just counting the seconds until I could finally stand before the judge. I hadn't heard anything from anyone about my case. I didn't know if I had gotten approved for a lawyer through that service I signed up with. No one was telling me anything. It was frustrating. I was being eaten alive with worry and anxiety. I had grown tired of sitting in the same place, looking at the same faces, and I just wanted to get everything over with. But the courts were taking their dear sweet time, certainly a reminder of who's on whose time. I just had to wait until they got ready for me.

To combat the anxiety I was feeling, I kept myself busy reading the Bible. I continued to study it and learn it and grow in my understanding of God. It was either focus on my situation and go crazy or focus on God and maintain a sense of sanity, hope and optimism. I could either stress myself to death or rely on my faith. I realized why I needed the confirmation of the end at the beginning: I needed something to lean on when frustration, fear and discouragement crept in and attacked my mind. I had to repeat the words that were spoken over me by that minister and Keisha

CHAPTER 8: CRAZINESS

over and over again. I had to keep reminding myself that it would all be over soon and that I would come out as the winner. I couldn't image how much of a wreck I would have been had I not had a sense of hope in my heart. I think—I'm sorry, let me correct that: I know I would have snapped and lost my mind just like some of the other girls I was locked up with.

    The misery and loneliness that accompanies being locked up can have a profound effect on a person's mind. Again, even though you're surrounded by people, you still feel alone. The desperation to return to normal life grows within you like a fungus; it builds like the pressure from a tea kettle until finally, without warning, it blows your lid off and you snap. Looking back, that's the only way I can describe what happened to one girl who was locked up with me at York. She was quiet and was always to herself. She never got in any trouble, messed with anyone, ticked off the correctional officers, or showed any signs of losing it. But one day, while we were all eating, she went crazy. She just lost it and began screaming, yelling, and pounding her fist on the table. Everyone was shocked. We were taken by surprise. She had become a totally different person. Thankfully, at the time there was a correctional officer on duty named Ms. Sharon. She was firm, but respectful towards the inmates. She wasn't the type to talk to us like we were dogs. She treated us like human beings. She dealt gently and kindly with the girl. Had there been another correctional officer dealing with the matter, that girl would have been surrounded by heavily armored guards, then thrown to the ground before being strapped down or stripped naked and put in solitary confinement where she would have completely lost it. Prison guards aren't trained nor are they encouraged to meet pain with kindness, to bring comfort to broken hearts, to be a listening ear and bring relief to the distraught; they are only trained to maintain order using brute force and prevent someone from killing another or themselves. They will leave you alone to deal with your own emotions. That's prison: cold and unsympathetic; mechanical and soul-less. That's no place to have a mental health crisis, although it's set up to make you do just that. Therefore, when you find a spark of kindness in there, be thankful for it because it doesn't have to be there. That's why I was thankful for Sharon. She was like an angel to many of us, a subtle reminder that this world still has some good in it.

    Ms. Sharon eventually got the girl to calm down. She talked to her and even allowed her cry on her shoulder. That girl had built up so much pressure and frustration inside of her that she could no longer compose herself. She was on the verge of losing her mind.

    When I saw that girl lose it, I teared up. I felt for her. I knew what she was feeling; I was feeling it. That same frustration was attempting to overtake me. If not for God, it would have. I just remember praying to God, "Lord, please don't let me go insane in here." The desperation in my voice caused it to shake. I could feel my body tensing up. For the rest of that day, I felt the heavy weight of anxiety bearing down on me. My nerves were jangly. My mind was spinning. But that night, like an ever-present friend, I heard the voice of God in a different way. This time, it wasn't the audible voice of an angel, nor was it the outside voice of a prophet,

CHAPTER 8: CRAZINESS

but it was in the form of an inner voice:

"I'm not only with you; I give you peace of mind."

That was my voice, but those weren't my words; I know because I don't talk like that. I never have. Today, I recognize what it was: it's what the Bible refers to as the "still, small voice" of God, whispering into our souls. Those words soothed me just like the lyrics to Plumb's song did. They took the edge away and brought me back down to a calm state. And they produced a different type of tear in my eyes—these were tears of joy rather than sadness. I knew I was going to be fine after that.

Like the poem *Footprints* says, during those times when you cannot stand and walk on your own, God is the one who carries you in His arms. I felt like I was being carried; better yet, I knew I was. I'd lost my strength some time back. And the journey still wasn't over. In fact, my long journey through my legal battle was just getting started.

Journal entries documenting my dreams and my journey

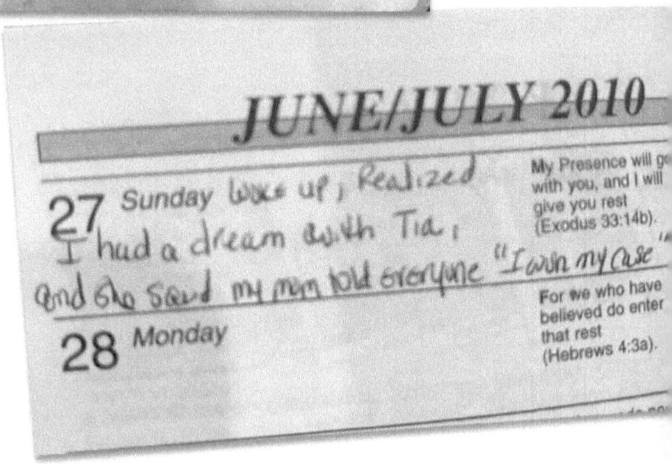

JUNE/JULY 2010

27 Sunday Woke up, Realized I had a dream with Tia, and she said my mom told everyone "I won my case"

28 Monday

My Presence will go with you, and I will give you rest (Exodus 33:14b).

For we who have believed do enter that rest (Hebrews 4:3a).

Chapter 9
THE BASTARD OUT OF BROOKLYN

I WAS TRANSFERRED FROM CAMBRIA BACK TO YORK County Prison—that's where the immigration judges were. There were two immigration judges. The one presiding over my case was Judge Durling. I remember before my trial finally got underway, I wrote the judge a letter explaining my situation to him. I apologized for my crimes and explained to him that I didn't know about the rules pertaining to green card holders since I was only five-years-old when I came to this country. I also explained to him that I have six kids and that I really wanted to be in their lives, that the US was the only place I'd ever called home, and I was a US citizen through my mother. I poured my heart out in that letter, hoping it would help my case. But once I stood in front of that judge for the first time, I felt the cold draft of his indifference as he wouldn't even acknowledge the letter.

The other immigration judge, Judge Arthur, was very

lenient towards inmates. He was the complete opposite of Judge Durling. He often granted Cancellation of Removal requests to inmates who'd been ordered deported. What that meant was those inmates would be given another chance to remain in the country as long as they didn't break the law and get locked up. He gave so many girls a chance to stay here after they were already ordered deported, but most of them couldn't resist the temptation of the streets. I would see many of them return through those revolving doors right after being released. They would get out of jail, stay clean for a day or two, and then go right back to doing what got them locked up the first time. Some of them even had the nerve to complain that the system was unfair towards them. I would be like, *Girl, they just released you and gave you a second chance. Why did you do what you did? Why did you go back and start shoplifting? You're the one who screwed up!* Those girls had it easy. They stood before the nice judge. But me, I had the mean judge, the one with a reputation for granting not one Cancellation of Removal order and who loved to send inmates away. I knew this was going to be a fight.

I hadn't heard back from the group that offered the attorney services pro bono, so I was prepared to represent myself during my hearing. And I came prepared. I spent most of my time in the prison library researching Immigration laws and past cases. I was even doing research and printing out information for other inmates who had cases, helping them out. That's when I started to understand what the correctional officers and judges deal with. A few of the women I helped were genuine and sincere like this Jamaican girl whose situation was life-threatening. Her community

CHAPTER 9: THE BASTARD OUT OF BROOKLYN

was run by a gang who threatened to murder her and her family if she didn't submit to their demands. The authorities in that area seemed powerless against that gang, and that's why she fled that country and insisted on remaining in the United States. However, there was another lady I was helping who wasn't very honest. This girl claimed to be in danger in her homeland, but what she was really doing was crafting and making up her story along the way. She had me looking up cases so that she could use those backstories as her own, hoping to gain sympathy from the judge with a make-believe threat. She came up with the lie that her village in Africa where she was from was raided by a group of men who gang-raped her before murdering her family before her eyes, and she claimed that if she was sent back to her country those men would kill her. Her entire story was a lie.

Another inmate pretended to go insane to avoid deportation. This girl pooped into her hand, and then smeared it all over the walls. Because of her, we were all placed on lockdown for two days. Everyone was pissed off. That same girl later approached me and asked me to help her with her case, but she was lying and playing games, making up stuff and being untruthful with me. I had seen other girls do stuff like fake a sickness so that they could get pills, and then they overmedicate themselves so they could actually become sick and avoid being sent away. I saw all kinds of stuff while operating in the role of the unofficial prison lawyer for many of these girls.

*

Normally, I would keep my business to myself and not share

the details of my case with others. I found it unwise to ask others about their personal business as well. You see, when it comes to immigration laws, two people can be locked up for the same thing but receive different verdicts. Sometimes girls would get together and talk about their crimes. They would be like, *Yeah, girl, I got locked up for that too. Yeah, girl, I did that too.* But then, jealousy would creep in when one girl discovered that another girl had a better chance of remaining in the US. And it could be a small thing that makes the difference: one girl has a better lawyer, or one girl's parents were US citizens and the other girl's parents aren't. Jealousy could lead to conflicts and confrontations, and these things could land you in the hole or ruin your chances of beating your case.

As immigrant inmates, we were already having problems with the inmates that were US citizens by birth; it was a case of the immigrant inmates verses the American inmates. American inmates didn't like the fact that the immigrant inmates were treated better than them. We were given special privileges the American inmates were given. For example, we were allowed to have special hair products; the other inmates weren't. We weren't roughed up like the other inmates by the correctional officers. We received free calls unlike the others, and we received better food. If we were sick or in need, the correctional officers would respond to us a lot quicker than they would the other inmates. We were given double sheets and pillows, and more.

There would regularly be arguments between the immigrant inmates and the American inmates. The Americans would often shout at us, "Why don't you go back to your

CHAPTER 9: THE BASTARD OUT OF BROOKLYN

country!" If the Americans wanted better food or needed medicine, often times they would ask us to appeal to the correctional officers on their behalves. Although we were inmates like the Americans, we were treated like special guests in the prison.

I would get involved with the other girls' cases when they came to me for help. Because I was a pod-worker, I had access to the prison library and certain services unlike the others. Even still, while helping others to beat their cases, I had doubts and fears concerning my case. To be honest, the odds were stacked against me. Due to my initial sentence, I was a prime candidate for deportation. According to the courts, if an immigrant receives a sentence of six months or more behind bars, they are supposed to be deported automatically. If an immigrant gets locked up for a crime but receives a sentence of six months or less, they are ineligible for deportation. I was given a six month prison sentence with an additional seventeen months of probation. In the eyes immigration officials, probation time still counts as prison time. Therefore, I had earned an automatic deportation.

I also learned that had both of my parents become US citizens before my eighteenth birthday, I would have been registered as a US citizen. My mom became a US citizen before my thirteenth birthday, but Walter didn't become one until after my eighteenth birthday; therefore I missed that deadline.

And like I mentioned earlier, I got stuck with the meanest and most merciless judge. He had no compassion. So things weren't looking too good for me.

FACE THE MUSIC

LOOKING BAD

My first court appearance finally came. I was scared, but prepared. At the time, I didn't have a lawyer to represent me, so for the first couple of appearances I had to represent myself. Later, I learned the paperwork I filled out for an attorney went through and I was assigned a lawyer pro bono. And as time went by, after four court hearings with my pro bono lawyer, then I was granted what is known as a merit hearing, which is a hearing where a non-citizen receives the chance to present arguments before an immigration judge and defend his or her right to remain in the United States.

At the merit hearing, the court interviewed me and asked if I knew who my biological father was. I told them I didn't know who he was, which was true. I was convinced of that after overhearing my mom and Walter argue over me on that fateful night. Never did I imagine that what turned out to be devastating news would later turn out to be good news.

Not too long after my merit hearing, several court sessions later, the court interviewed my mom. They asked her about my biological father's identity. She confirmed that Walter wasn't my real father, but her following statements left everyone even more confused. As I discovered after my lawyer provided me with a copy of the transcript of her testimony, my mom provided the court with one story concerning the possible identity of my biological dad—she told me and my sisters something totally different from what she told the court.

The story she told the court was my dad was a Puerto Rican seller she met and had sexual relations with. Accord-

CHAPTER 9: THE BASTARD OUT OF BROOKLYN

ing to her, it was a one-night-stand—I was the product of it. But she then flipped her story and shared with the court something totally different.

The story she told me she was living in Panama, and at one point, she was in an abusive relationship. She tried to escape the abusive relationship by moving into a cheap place—it was a room that was connected to a gas station. While there, she had no way to bathe her three kids. She barely had any food to feed them. So one day, she went downstairs to the gas station attendant and asked him if she could use his facilities to bathe her kids. He agreed on one condition: she have sex with him. She went through with his offer and I was the result of that union. After discovering she was pregnant, she informed the man of her condition and he simply gave her a hundred dollars and told her to "get rid of it."

Her last story was similar to the first two; it entailed a one-night-stand with a stranger in some seedy location. I was the result thereof.

I was just as confused as the judge must have been while beholding that testimony. My lawyer told me before supplying me with a copy of the transcript that the court made my mom look pretty bad, like she was a wild and loose woman. Maybe that was the case. However, there was so much riding on the line for me. I couldn't afford to care about how the truth made my mother looked. If we didn't get this thing right, it was adios amigos for me. My children would most likely never see their mother again. I couldn't afford for that to happen.

OUT FOR BLOOD

It was unfortunate that Walter had passed before I got locked up. It was unfortunate for me because, according to US immigration law, he was the key to my freedom. We needed his saliva to prove I wasn't his daughter. Now, there was no chance of us getting his blood since he was no longer with us. However, there was still a way to work around that.

Walter had one living sister left, my aunt. This particular aunt reached out to me after I let it be known that Walter wasn't my biological father. She was actually supportive of me during my ordeal, which was good because I needed her to provide her DNA to the court so we could definitively prove that me and Walter were not related. I reached out to her to help me in this regard, writing her a letter stating what I needed her to do, but sadly, she never got that letter—her daughter threw it away. I felt handicapped by that.

Since my aunt failed to come through for me, I had to move to the next best thing: I had to get a few of my siblings to submit their DNA to the lab for testing. Thankfully, they agreed. They provided their DNA to the lab and then we all sat back and waited for the results.

After a few days, the results came in. I could hardly contain my excitement. I was super nervous also, hoping they confirmed what I'd suspected for many years—that Walter wasn't my real dad. For if they did, I was going to be a free woman.

That's it! I did it! I just proved beyond a shadow of a doubt that Walter is not my father! Hallelujah! That's all I could think when the results were read. It was conclusive: Walter wasn't my father. I was jumping up and down like a

CHAPTER 9: THE BASTARD OUT OF BROOKLYN

guest on the Maury Show. I felt like I did it, I beat the case. The percentages were extremely high that I wasn't related to Walter. My siblings and I didn't share the same father. I was ready to take my victory lap then. However, the prosecution wouldn't let me off so easily.

"Your honor, these results do not prove that Mr. Dehaney isn't the defendant's father; this could mean that Mr. Dehaney is the defendant's biological father and not her siblings'."

"You've got to be kidding," I murmured under my breath. "This guy can't be serious." I thought I had this one won, but the prosecutor was able to flip the evidence around and make it work to his advantage. So now, I was stuck, forced to find another way to prove I was not the biological child of a man who, at the time of my birth, wasn't a US citizen. Back to the drawing board.

MARCH 2011

13 Sunday

Seek the LORD while He may be found, call upon Him while He is near (Isaiah 55:6). 731

14 Monday

The LORD is good to those who wait for Him, to the soul who seeks Him (Lamentations 3:25). 732

15 Tuesday Court @ 9am. Nothing really - courts been regular these days. I already know what's what.

He who comes to God must believe that He is, and ... a rewarder of those who diligently seek Him (Hebrews 11:6b). 733

16 Wednesday Called Lourdes Told her to send Melissa the papers.

And you will seek Me and find Me, when you search for Me with all your heart (Jeremiah 29:13). 734

17 Thursday We got locked down because someone pooped in th shower.

I love those who love me, and those who seek me diligently will find me (Proverbs 8:17). 73

18 Friday

Cleared 2day.

Ask, and it will be given to you; seek, and you will find; knock, and it will be opened to you (Matthew 7:7). 73

19 Saturday INS phone call Spoke to Melissa & Mary. for some reason talkn to Melissa 2day was diffrnt. I felt good. HAPPY I could't ~

But seek first the kingdom of God and His righteousness, and all these things shall be added to you (Matthew 6:33). 73

102

Chapter 10
THE SCARIEST DAY OF MY LIFE

E VERY IMMIGRANT INMATE FACING DEPORTATION feared that dreaded 4 am wake up call. They knew what that meant. It meant they were officially being transferred to one of the drop-off spots for deportation. The way it happened was the officers would wake up the immigrant inmates who had officially been ordered deported. They would instruct them to collect their belongings and then transport them to a special holding cell where they would await the transportation vehicle that was coming to get them. Once on that bus, those inmates were taken to another prison in Texas. *Why Texas?* It's because Texas was closest to the border; it was the final stop before being put on a plane and flown out of the country. And once gone, there was no coming back.

Many nights, I barely sleep due to anxiety. I was worried that I was going to receive that dreaded 4 am call.

FACE THE MUSIC

It felt like Judge Durling was playing around with me, giving me a bunch of seemingly impossible demands. First, I proved through DNA—at least, I thought I did—that I was unrelated to Walter, that my real father was still unknown. My mom even confirmed this in her sworn testimony along with mine. What more did I need? According to the judge, I needed a lot more, something even more concrete than DNA.

This was starting to get tiring. I was becoming worn-out by all of the back and forth. My lawyer and I were doing all we could to overturn my case, but it was beginning to look like our efforts were futile. It was as if this judge was out for blood—my blood. Just when I thought I had provided enough evidence of my citizenship, the judge upped the ante and made it much more difficult for me with a new set of demands. My attorney and I were filing one appeal after another just trying to stay in the game. And all the while, the possibility that we might lose this case loomed ever so closer over my head. Time was running out for us.

I was putting in work in the prison library, spending hours looking up laws and cases to help my case. Practically, I was doing all of the work for my lawyer. Even he suggested that I be a paralegal; it seemed natural to me. But truthfully, I was just driven and desperate. I had to win because there was so much riding on this case for me.

And, as if the stress of a difficult courtroom battle wasn't enough, I still *had to deal with the everyday challenges of life in prison. Stay out of trouble, Antoinette. Don't sweat the small stuff*, Antoinette. Girl, don't pay her any mind; she's just jealous. I had to keep my head on straight and avoid

CHAPTER 10: THE SCARIEST DAY OF MY LIFE

potentially harmful situations that could have landed me in even deeper and hotter waters.

In prison, small things can lead to big problems. Resentment and anger are like cancers: they start out small before metastasizing. And if not careful, you could end up somewhere you don't want to be: in the hole, or worst: in the morgue. But I was too close to the end to let little grievances derail me. I had a goal, which was to get out of there, and nobody was going to get in my way.

DEESCALATION

I remember this Jamaican girl named Alesia; we were good friends. Both of us were in the same boat, battling just to remain in America. Now, I prided myself on avoiding drama and staying out of trouble, but I'll admit that even I had my limitations. The two of us nearly got into it. Had things escalated to a high level, this would have cost me my job as a pod-worker, where I had access to the prison library. Not only that, but both of us could have ended up in the hole.

Looking back, the whole situation was petty. I was talking with some of the ladies about my family and showing them pictures of my kids. Every time I would brag about something my kids had, Alesia would cut in and brag that her kids had the same stuff. It was as if she wanted all of the attention. She was competing with me. Whenever I would brag on something I had, she would do the same and then try to prove she had more. Finally, I had enough. I confronted her, asking her why she wanted so much attention. She started to get loud with me, so I started to get loud with her.

Normally, whenever the correctional officers see two

inmates arguing, they immediately jump into action and send in the tactical team; they don't wait until an argument escalates into a fist fight. That's what could have happened to us, but thankfully, the officer on duty at that time was a lady named Ms. Kim.

    Ms. Kim had a lot of respect for me. She knew my character, that I wasn't the type to cause a lot of drama. She perceived me as being mature. Of course, throughout the course of a day, you may get upset with people, you might even become irate, but using wisdom, you consider the consequences of bad actions before doing something drastic and stupid. A wise person thinks about everything they have to lose before throwing everything away just to protect their pride. I didn't have time to act like a fool. I just wanted to let Alesia know I was tired of what she was doing to me. I shared with her my feelings and deescalated the situation by lowering my tone. From there, what began as an argument turned into a discussion. Then Ms. Kim said to everyone, "Ya'll hear this? Now, that is an adult conversation taking place, and you guys need to take notice of that!" And she was telling the truth: we handled the situation like adults. Sure, the situation wasn't petty, but egos are easily provoked. The simplest things can trigger people, especially when they're already under a lot of stress. All of us were on edge. And it would have been easy for me to simply bury resentment in my heart towards Alesia, then go back to cell as if nothing happened, all the while letting that resentment fester and eat away at me until I can no longer take it anymore. That's when we do stupid things. Instead, I decided to talk through my feelings, get it out in the open, release any negative emo-

CHAPTER 10: THE SCARIEST DAY OF MY LIFE

tions I was carrying, and then move on.

IT'S TOO LATE

"Antoinette, get up and pack your things! It's time for you to go!"

"Wha—What? What's going on? It's time to go?" I looked at the officer with a look of disbelief. *It was 4 am.* "No! *This can't be happen*ing," I muttered. I still have time. They can't do this to me!

It was too late. Judge Durling finally issued the order for me to be deported. Time was up. It appeared as if nothing could be done to stop or reverse his decision. My heart sank into my stomach. I felt my strength fleeting, leaving me weak and lethargic. Eventually, I collected myself and began gathering my things. I was so disappointed I wanted to burst out in tears, but I held it in like usual. It wouldn't have done any good anyway—tears weren't going to stop me from boarding that bus to Texas. After gathering my stuff, I was led by the officer to a holding location where several girls were waiting. This was the final stop before boarding the bus out of town and then out of the country.

When I entered the room, I could see the desperation in all of their eyes. It didn't matter that they were acting like they weren't scared, even pretending to make light of the situation; they were scared just like me. Some of them were terrified, and they had every right to be. America was that great beacon of freedom, that big bastion of opportunity. But back in some of their countries, they would have to go back to no opportunities, extreme poverty; they would have to face the most wicked gangs, warlords who were allowed to rage indiscriminately and freely, certain death and more. Some of them had to go back to communist governments that hoarded all of the food and supplies and micromanaged people's lives among other things, and they would have to say goodbye to their families here in the US. Some would be sent to strange lands where they would have to completely learn a new culture and set of customs.

My eyes held a look of weariness and defeat. I was tired of trying, furthermore, tired of hoping and believing things would turn around. I didn't see any evidence of a turnaround—no good news, no breakthrough moments where it appeared as if my judge was going to make an about-face. He seemed hell-bent on sending me away, and now he'd won. I was done.

I just gave up at that moment. I can't say I was content with the judge's decision—I was angry, resentful, and I felt deeply wronged as if the victim of a grave injustice. But what could I do? Nothing! All I could do was swallow it, and then tell myself I'll eventually be okay. I'll learn how to live with it...someday.

But what about God in all of this; where was He? Did He abandon His promise? Or did He forget His promise? I'd had my hopes up; they were sitting above the clouds. But as the case drew on, day after day, my hopes were dropping lower and lower. I thought that I still had a chance in the final stretch, in the final round, but now the fight was over and I was declared the loser. What happened? Did I not have enough faith? Did I do something wrong?

I so desperately wanted to hear that still, small voice in my soul again, but I didn't hear a thing. It was as if God

CHAPTER 10: THE SCARIEST DAY OF MY LIFE

went radio-silence on me. I certainly wasn't expecting one of these girls to look up and say something comforting to me; they appeared to be on pins and needles and needed a great deal of encouragement themselves. *God, where are you?* I wondered, staring up at the ceiling. I continued to fight back the tears that eagerly tried to escape from my eyes. I simply needed some sign that God was still with me, if He ever was to begin with.

*

I was playing it tough but trembling with fear. I was holding it together on the surface, but the sound of that cell door being unlocked from the outside caused my nerves to become unglued. Every time I heard that click-clack, that meant an officer was coming to take one or several of us away and to the bus to be transported to our final drop-off destination before being flown out of the country: Texas. We dreaded being on that bus. To many of us, that was the long bus-ride to Hell.

Click-clack! The cell door opened and an officer summoned more girls. As waves of girls exited, it felt like the room got a little bit smaller. It was certainly quieter. I was thinking about my children and how I would miss them so. I thought about my siblings and how much fun we used to have running all over the neighborhood. It was like my life was being projected onto a big movie screen in my head. Usually, people see their lives flash before their eyes before taking their final breath; all I could see flashing before my eyes were mistakes I wish I could have gone back in time to avoid and images of a possible future that terrified me.

FACE THE MUSIC

After several minutes, we heard the door being unlocked. *Click-clack!* The door swung open, and standing in its entrance was a stone-faced guard pointing his index finger. "You, you, and you, I need you to come with me!" Now, the rest of the girls were gone. Suddenly, I found myself all alone, cold and feeling sad. I was sitting with my eyes closed and waiting for my turn to be called.

Time was ticking away and I was just sitting there, but it felt like time was just standing still. I felt like holding my breath at times. The silence was like a prison cell; it was foreboding like an ominous omen. God, why don't these people just come and get me and get it over! I'm tired of sitting here waiting. Come on! Come on! I inwardly complained.

Finally, after a while, I heard the click-clack of the door. "Thank God!" I murmured as I exhaled a sigh of relief. I was just ready to leave. I was ready to get it over with. I didn't want to wait another second in that cold cell for what was already inevitable. But the officer that stood in the doorway didn't say anything to me; he just stared at me with a puzzled expression on his face. He then looked at another officer and asked, "What's going on with this one?"

"I don't know. Apparently, they made a mistake. She has to go back," the other officer answered. The officer took me back upstairs to my cell and apologized for the mishap. My head was swirling with confusion and a sense of jubilation. I didn't know what went wrong, but I was glad it did go wrong. That bought me some more time. Or, so I hoped.

Once I got back to my cell, I rushed and contacted my lawyer to find out if he knew what just happened. He

CHAPTER 10: THE SCARIEST DAY OF MY LIFE

was as clueless as could be. He said he'd look into the matter and then get back to me as soon as possible.

My fear at that moment was that another officer was going to come by my cell and tell me they didn't make a mistake the first time and that I was supposed to be on that bus, and then move me again to that waiting cell. I was praying that didn't happen. That's all I could do. So, again, I just sat and waited, hoping for good news at last while preparing for the worse.

JANUARY 2011

9 Sunday I had the most wonderful dream. I dreamt I went home and surprised LeeHad N Nico. OMG, I want this dream to come true so bad.

We love Him because He first loved us (1 John 4:19).

668

10 Monday Court @ 1pm Court was okay, but that birth certificate is really needed.

You shall love the Lord your God with all your heart, with all your soul, and with all your mind

66

MARCH 2011

738 **20 Sunday** Had a dream I was Released.
Mailed the Envelope to Melissa
Got off Lockdown 2day.

Then Jesus came and spoke to them, saying, All authority has been given to Me in heaven and on earth (Matthew 28:18).

739 **21 Monday** 19 mnths with immigration.

O LORD, You are our Father; we are the clay, and You our potter; and all we are the work of Your hand (Isaiah 64:8b

112

Chapter 11
EMANCIPATION

Judge Durling's order had been overturned by the Board of Immigration Appeals (BIA) at the last minute. Normally, the BIA doesn't take interlocutory cases, which was what my case was; but it just so happened they decided to take my case. They determined that they didn't find Judge Durling's decision to be relevant because for a child to derive citizenship through their parents, both parents need to be biological according to American law; therefore, if the child is illegitimate, which, in my case meant my biological father never filed taxes on me or tried to be in my life, then he could not be ruled as my biological father.

My lawyer later discovered what the issue was with Judge Durling. Concerning my case, he wasn't relying on US immigration laws to sway his decision; he was using Panamanian laws to sway his decision. There I was, looking up US immigration laws and making sure I went by the book while he was playing by a different set of rules. Oh, I was irate.

FACE THE MUSIC

According to Panamanian law, a man can be considered a child's legal father even if he isn't the biological father. As long as that man files for taxes on that child and seeks to be in his or her life in any way, he is considered by their government as the father. Again, it doesn't work that way in America. If we had been relying on American immigration laws the whole time, I would have beaten my case at the very beginning and gone free. But I had to rot in prison month after month for nearly two-and-a-half-years. Each time my court appearance was rescheduled, I had to wait months before standing before the judge again. Every time my lawyer filed an appeal, I had to fill out a mountain of paperwork. It was exhausting to say the least.

The BIA gave Judge Durling thirty-days to respond to their decision. They had everything I could offer them, a mountain of evidence supporting my claim to US citizenship. Now the ball was in our court it seemed—someone more powerful than the judge had stepped and overruled his decision. And that was totally unexpected.

Even though my attorney and I had made a game-changing discovery, we still had to keep our fingers crossed. We dared not take this judge lightly. We were grateful that he now had heat on his back from a higher source, but anything could happen. We still weren't out of the water. So I had to continue to play it safe.

*

The day went just like any other day. Breakfast first thing in the morning, then back to our cells for role-call. After that, everyone had to get busy doing what they were assigned to

CHAPTER 11: EMANCIPATION

do. I had a new job—I was responsible for overseeing the laundry room. Of course, this led to me having a new nickname given to me by one of the correctional officers named Ms. Kim: Bubbles. On a side note: Ms. Kim was real cool with me, and we're still cool to this very day. I remember when she passed by my bunk one day and saw me resting; she told me I looked like I was so peaceful at the time. Her words were so encouraging to me; they revealed that sometimes, in the midst of the craziness all around us, the peace of God which rests on our lives shines like a light in the darkness. In essence, my faith inspired her. You never know who's watching you.

But back to the laundry incident. While working in the laundry room, I would collect what I could only describe as mesh-bags. These bags would be filled with the inmates' clothes. We never pulled out the clothes or sorted through them; our job was to take the entire bag and throw it into the washing machine as is. Some of the girls would sneak extra cleaning detergent into the bags with their clothes in hopes of getting their clothes extra clean. So the laundry room workers would find themselves oftentimes adding detergent to bags that already had detergent in them, and this would cause the machines to be overrun with bubbles. While cleaning out the bubbles one day, that's when Ms. Kim saw me, and hence, the nickname.

Now, in prison, anything can be counted as contraband. Contraband isn't always what people think it is; it can be something as simple as having an extra pillow or blanket, or taking a banana or some other piece of food to your cell. Harboring contraband can earn you a trip to the hole.

FACE THE MUSIC

Of course, I can understand the necessity of such drastic measures when considering some of the people I was locked up with. Inmates who wanted to harm themselves or others were known to hide things under their pillows and mattresses. They would hide things in other places as well that I don't want to go into detail about.

One day, I took something simple with me back to my bunk. It was nothing harmful. Again, simple things like a piece of fruit of an extra pillow is considered contraband. I knew that the consequences were severe if it was discovered that I'd taken something back with me to my cell. The COs were known to carry out spontaneous bunk-checks where they would make inmates stand by while they check their bunks, flipping over mattresses and looking in every nook and cranny for contraband. And they wouldn't tell anyone when they were coming; they would simply surprise us. They would also check our bunks when we weren't present.

I took something back to my bunk that wasn't allowed, thinking it was harmless and that it shouldn't have been a big deal. But I was also terrified, thinking I was going to get caught. The thought of that jacked my heart-rate up tremendously. I didn't want to jeopardize my position and good standing over something as simple as a piece of fruit or a donut or something. Again, I sensed that I was at the end of the road and couldn't afford to start messing up.

*

I was busy doing the laundry when suddenly, my name was called. I recognized the call. It was a correctional officer. They speak in an intimidating and authoritative manner.

CHAPTER 11: EMANCIPATION

"Antoinette, I need you to stop what you're doing and follow me," the officer ordered.

Oh, crap, they found my stuff. I'm screwed. I nervously stopped what I was doing and went with the officer. *I can't believe it—my first time in the hole. And for what? Why did I have to be such an idiot? God, please get me out of this. I promise I won't do that ever again if you do.*

With each step, my body tensed up. I began to feel queasy, nauseous. Pressure gripped my head like a vice-grip. They were leading me back to the section where my cell was. I knew I'd been discovered now. I was in trouble.

When we walked through the door leading to the dorm section, I was met with screaming, cheering, and a thunderous applause as all of the girls there were celebrating me. I had no clue what was going on. What was this all about?

I heard ladies shouting, "Congratulations! You're free! You're free!"

"What? What do you mean I'm free?" I asked one of the girls.

"They didn't tell you? You didn't see the letter?"

"What letter?" I asked. I asked the officer what was going on, and she presented me with a letter from the immigration court stating that I had won my case. I hit the ground in tears. It had been years in the making, years of me battling it out, going back and forth with the courts, and now, I was officially free.

"You deserve it!" several of the ladies shouted as they reigned down pats and back rubs. I began to thank God. These tears were full of joy and gladness. I didn't believe that day would ever come. I didn't. I had given up hope. And now, it was all over.

I won!

*

If I'm dreaming, don't wake me up. That's all I could think. But it wasn't a dream; it was really happening. I was being set free. And like a free woman, I began giving away all of my things to the other ladies. I was still teary-eyed as they were wishing me well. It felt surreal.

On November 23, 2011, I finally became a free woman. That was the day I walked out of that prison and never looked back.

*

To this very day, I still keep in contact with several of the ladies from the two prisons I was in. I keep in contact with Keisha, the girl who prophesied to me that I would win my case. I keep in touch with some of the correctional officers I'd come to know and befriend. For example, one of the officers is a woman named Moniecca. She used to call me O.N.S., a nickname that stood for "one night stand." She called me that because she was familiar with my story. After I got released, she would ask me to look up cases and information that could help the other girls during their trials. It's awesome how much some of the COs actually care about the inmates. To me, she was amazing.

I look back on those years and think about a lot of those ladies. They became my family. Some of them died while in prison, some of them got deported, and some of

CHAPTER 11: EMANCIPATION

them got released. We still talk to this day on social media. However, my heart aches for every person that enters those revolving doors; and more for those embroiled in the immigration battle. I experienced being locked up as a US citizen and being locked up as an immigrant. I know the stresses and the pains they both bring. I know how tough it is when inmates are trying to maintain a sense of hope and sanity in the midst of all of the craziness. But I also know that faith in God is what makes the only difference.

I can't overstate how critical faith in God is especially when facing obstacles that are too big to conquer. There is a power greater than any power on this earth. There is invisible help all around you: God, the invisible one, the one who said He would be a Father to us, a protector, a friend, a provider and a guide.

He sought me. He got me right where He wanted me and then called my name. The interesting thing is He was pursuing me when I didn't know Him, when He was just an afterthought in my mind. Like the Bible says,

> "We love him, because he first loved us." (1 John 4:19, KJV)

I'm so glad He made Himself known to me in those midnight hours and on those days when I was too lost to follow Him. I wouldn't have made it without that experiential knowledge of Him. I would have died, either instantly by suicide or slowly by hopelessness and despair. But I made it. I overcame the insurmountable and conquered what I wouldn't have been able to conquer on my own. My lawyer,

FACE THE MUSIC

although good, couldn't have brought me to this point. And my family, although loving, weren't able to do anything for me. God set it up where I had nowhere to turn; that way, I had no other choice but to turn to Him. Now I turn to Him for everything. Although not perfect—no one really is—I recognize that I'm never alone, and that I have a "refuge and strength, an ever-present help in trouble" (Psalm 46:1, NIV).

Like me, it's your job to turn to Him. Call upon Him. He's listening. He wants to meet you right where you are and rescue you. His name is Jesus.

UNFINISHED BUSINESS

When I walked out of that prison, there was no one there to pick me up. I was in Pennsylvania, too far from home. Thankfully, my attorney was nice enough to purchase me a bus ticket back to New York. I had money on my books, but prisons never give you cash; they simply give you a check once released. So I was grateful for his assistance.

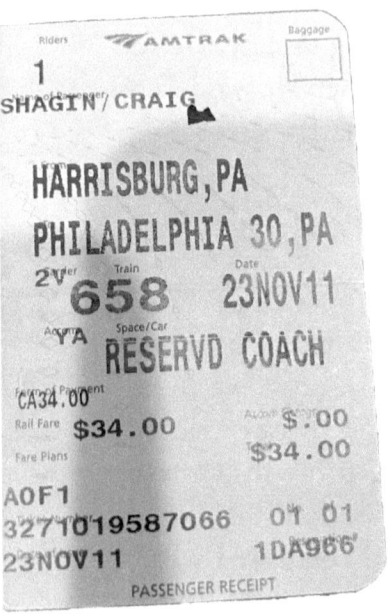

I remember sitting in the bus station, waiting for my bus, and thinking, *What if they say, 'We made a mistake. Antoinette is supposed to be deported.' And then they change their minds and come for me at the station.* Fear started speaking to me, putting all kind of thoughts in my head. I wasn't aware of something called Spiritual Warfare, which is where

CHAPTER 11: EMANCIPATION

the enemy of all mankind, Satan, tries to attack and rule our hearts and minds using thoughts and emotions like fear. In those moments, we have to remind ourselves of God's love for us and rehearse what God told us and tells us in His Word (the Bible) rather than entertain those fearful thoughts. I began to learn about that later on in life. I'll save that for another book. But for now, let's just say the battle was over, the victory had been won, and it was time for me to take my victory lap, not imprison myself with irrational fears. It was time to breathe the fresh air and bask in the freedom I'd gained.

*

Of course, there was still some unfinished business I needed to attend to. I wanted to get my identity right on paper. So I hired an attorney in Panama to assist me in getting Walter's last name off of my birth certificate and replacing it with my mother's maiden name, Mitchell. That went through successfully. And speaking of my mother...

*

I was excited about seeing everyone. The first thing I did once I got back home was hug and kiss my children. All of the little things that people take for granted, I wasn't planning on missing out on, not this time. I wanted to sit on the floor and watch movies with them, take them out for ice cream, and do everything else I dreamed about doing with them while I was away from them. It felt like Heaven feeling their little arms wrapped around me and feeling their beating hearts pressed against my body.

I was glad to see everyone: my siblings, and also my mother. I missed her. Yes, I was still upset with her, but I missed her. She was my mother and I still loved her. However, I carried in my heart the sting of her betrayal. From my childhood, that pain had been nagging at me. What I longed for most of all from her was a sense of closure.

I'd forgiven Walter in my heart for the things he said and did to me. I wasn't about to go through Hell only to get out and allow Hell to control my mind. I wanted peace, not war. Life is too precious to waste, relationships too valuable to destroy, but there are some questions we take with us to our graves. Sadly, the question of my biological father is one of those. My mom never disclosed to me who my real father was. I never knew why. I never understood why she would conceal that information from me in her heart, robbing me of something I desperately wanted.

I cannot honestly say I don't feel the need to know who my biological father is. Even to this day, the discussion comes up between my sisters and I. Of course, I'm a grown woman, but I'm still a human being with questions and a burning curiosity concerning my past. There are questions I want answered. I don't know if I'll ever get them in this lifetime. I might die with those questions burning in my heart, but if I do, I'll be okay. I've learned to live with the questions, to dance with the thorns in my side, to smile despite the pain, to live even when it feels like life isn't worth living.

This is the reality that all of us must live with. Many have gone on to become successful entertainers, actors, athletes, professionals, politicians and more despite feeling an overwhelming sense of emptiness as it pertains to under-

CHAPTER 11: EMANCIPATION

standing their pasts. They have gaps in their stories that have yet to be filled. Some were even raised in foster care homes and orphanages, abandoned and left at the doorsteps of complete strangers, sold by their parents for drugs, and worse.

But we weren't designed to live in the past. We were designed to live in the present moment while focusing on the future. That's where one's purpose is; it's where one's destiny lies.

I'm reminded of a famous Bible verse that reads, "'For I know the plans I have for you,' declares the LORD, 'plans to prosper you and not to harm you, plans to give you hope and a future'" (Jeremiah 29:11, NIV). Hope and a future; these are what God wants us to fix our eyes on. And it is for this reason I want to want to conclude my story with the following chapter.

FACE THE MUSIC

Chapter 12
CLOSURE

I'M NOT GOING TO LIE TO YOU AND CLAIM I DIDN'T FEEL hurt when thinking about my mom's actions. I also felt betrayed by her. I felt like she left a gaping wound in my heart and didn't care.

I wrestled with forgiveness for a while. Even after prison, I entered in and out of mental and emotional jail of bitterness. One minute, I was over what happened to me, and the next, I was angry and depressed by the memory of those things. One minute I would feel like I was on top of the world, and the next, I felt like I was being crushed under the weight of the world.

*

I thought often about the words that minister said to me at Lehigh, "You have to forgive." This was an ongoing battle for me. It was easier said than done in my mind. Perhaps, what made this so difficult was my belief. I believed I was owed something. I was owed an apology.

It was one thing to forgive someone who wronged me and then confessed their wrong, but it was another to forgive someone who wronged me and then pretended like they never did anything. In my mind, forgiveness was a superpower I held over others. I saw it as the power to set others free. If I withheld forgiveness from another, that was my way of punishing them for their crimes and trespasses. Little did I know the only one I was punishing was myself by being unforgiving.

As I'd done in prison, I continued to listen to Bible teachings from Christian ministers like Joyce Meyers and others. Just because I wasn't locked up, that didn't mean I could simply abandon the things that helped me to make it through. That's jail-house religion. I wasn't one who turned to God when going through and then abandoned Him when things got better. If I was going to serve God, I was going to be true to Him no matter what. That's what I'd always prided myself on. If I was with someone, I was with them, true to the end. I never wanted to be perceived as flaky. I wasn't about to start now. Anyway, how could I forget the incredible things I experienced of God while behind bars: the supernatural visitations; hearing God's voice; the prophecies and words of knowledge that were spoken over me. If anything, I was still curious as to how the whole spirit world worked. I still wanted answers to those questions. I never ended my spiritual quest for knowledge. And I'm still on it today.

But one of the habits I developed that was positive was listening to Christian teachings. If there was one thing I could control, it was what I listened to. I continued to listen

CHAPTER 12: CLOSURE

to music from Christian artists, uplifting and encouraging songs. I never stopped doing these things. I'm glad I kept that practice going because it was just as helpful outside of prison as it was inside of prison. It helped me to find freedom in my heart and soul.

Sometimes, you just have to change your playlist. Music that stirs up anger and hatred doesn't help you to find freedom from the demons that torment you at night. And best believe me when I say that unforgiveness opens the door for tormenting spirits in your life. You cannot be at rest when you're harboring revenge and bitterness towards others in your heart. Those things will consume you until they ultimately destroy you. Like one person put it, harboring unforgiveness is like drinking acid while hoping the other person dies. That's insane!

It took hearing minister after minister hammer over and over again the truth about forgiveness before I caught on to what they were saying. And here's the truth about forgiveness in a nutshell:

THE TRUTH ABOUT FORGIVENESS

When you forgive, you're not releasing the other person off the hook; you're setting yourself free. You see, justice will always be served in this world. I know some people don't believe that. I will agree that it doesn't look like that's the case, but trust me, it is. You know why? The Bible explains why in 2 Corinthians 5:10. It says,

"For we must all stand before Christ to be judged. We will each receive whatever we deserve for the good or evil we have done in this earthly body." (NLT)

Also, Romans 12:19-20 says,

> "Dear friends, never take revenge. Leave that to the righteous anger of God. For the Scriptures say, 'I will take revenge; I will pay them back,' says the LORD. Instead, 'If your enemies are hungry, feed them. If they are thirsty, give them something to drink. In doing this, you will heap burning coals of shame on their heads.'" (NLT)

Now, before you shout over the thought of that, consider this thought: You have done wrong just like others, so don't be so eager to see fire and brimstone fall on someone else's head so fast. Remember the mercy God showed you, and keep in mind that we all need that mercy.

Everyone sins. We all mess up. And according to the Bible, God sees everything we do. Nothing escapes His eyes. There are people who have committed heinous crimes against other people and have escaped detection and capture, but they didn't get away with anything because God saw them. Furthermore, their consciences saw everything. The Bible tells us in Romans 2:15 our own consciences will testify against us before God in judgement. That's scary because the conscience records not only our deeds, but our motives and intentions. Like Jesus said in Matthew 5:21-30, even if you hate someone in your heart or lust after someone in your heart, you've committed murder and adultery in

CHAPTER 12: CLOSURE

God's eyes. Your conscience is taking note of every thought and desire you entertain within.

And what's the punishment for being wicked? That's a good question. The Bible sums it up in one word: Hell. Hell means not only eternal separation from God in the afterlife, but it is also described as a place where its inhabitants will suffer and be burned eternally (Revelation 21:8; Matthew 13:50; Mark 9:43), a place where the body is tormented constantly and finds no rest (Revelation 14:11), a place where people will beg for a single drop of water but find none (Luke 16:9-31), and more. And the Bible doesn't depict Hell as a make-believe place, a figment of the imagination; it depicts Hell as a real, literal place.

Knowing this, I began to understand that God is not only a God of love; He is a God of justice. In His mercy, He gives us the chance to repent and turn to Him. He even sent His Son, Jesus, to die for our sins so that through His sacrifice our sins could be forgiven, and with His blood, our sins could be washed away. God loves us all. Salvation is free to us all. However, it is something we must choose to grab ahold of. God cannot force anyone to surrender to Him. So for those who choose to ignore God and continue to do evil in His sight, there's the alternative: Hell. God doesn't send people there; people send themselves there due to the hardness of their hearts.

The thought of that is scary. Actually, it began to breed compassion in my heart towards my mom and Walter. That's the one place I never want to see my family go, I don't care how much I may be upset with them. Hell isn't worth it. I wouldn't even wish that on my worse enemy. And apparently, it wasn't God's intention for anyone to go to that place either. Jesus said in Matthew 5:24 that God created Hell only for Satan and his angels, and not for man. But many people choose to go there.

I know the justice of God. I know how this thing works. So rather than fume in anger towards my mom, I began to pray for her. I began to pray for her healing from whatever it was that held her bound, bound enough to choose a man over her own daughter, bound enough to spiral down a pit of deception just to preserve secrets that I'm sure ate her alive. I wanted her to find the same peace and deliverance I found in Christ. I couldn't set her free. She had her own demons to fight. Only God could set her free, but I could pray for her. I understood that there was something bigger at stake than my own ego in this situation: the state of her soul. And I also knew that if I let bitterness and unforgiveness dominate me, then I would find myself in the judgement seat according to Matthew 6:15, which says, "But if you refuse to forgive others, your Father will not forgive your sins" (NLT).

No one and nothing is worth losing God and ending up in Hell over.

And you know, the thing about God is He knows how to humble us so that we right the wrongs we've committed towards others. He will never let a person remain hard-hearted. He is all about restoring relationships through honesty and transparency; that's His specialty.

*

Another thing about forgiveness is it frees you from the grip

CHAPTER 12: CLOSURE

of the past so that you can walk into your bright future. Again, unforgiveness only holds you back. You have to focus on your future—what you want to be, what you want to accomplish—and let that propel you forward in life. No one ever moved forward while constantly looking back.

God has a bright future for you. He wants to bless you and do incredible things in and through you (Jeremiah 29:11). He even wants you to pray to Him and ask Him to bless you in big ways as the prayer of Jabez 1 Chronicles 4:10 reveals. It reads, "Oh, that you would bless me and expand my territory! Please be with me in all that I do, and keep me from all trouble and pain!" The Bible says you have not because you ask not; so ask God to bless you mightily so you can turn around and bless others. It's His will to do it. He said it in Ephesians 3:20, which says, "Now all glory to God, who is able, through his mighty power at work within us, to accomplish infinitely more than we might ask or think" (NLT).

I'm saying this to you because I want you to understand that as a child of God, you have a very bright future ahead of you; you have a God who wants to bless you so magnificently that your past won't even compare to your future. He wants to "a crown of beauty for ashes, a joyous blessing instead of mourning, festive praise instead of despair" (Isaiah 61:3, NLT). That means He's going to make up for all of the trouble and pain you experienced.

But you have to forgive first.

*

What do you do with the pain? That's the question I pon-

FACE THE MUSIC

dered. I forgave my mother, but I still felt the pain of her betrayal; the same regarding Walter and others who hurt me. Two things:

1. Counseling. I know some people don't believe in counseling; they have too much pride. But it's important that you get with a skilled professional, whether it be a minister or therapist, and let them walk you through your painful experiences, helping you to process them. You can't go back and change the past; you can only process it so that it becomes less painful and you aren't as affected by it.
2. Use your pain to help others. Your pain is valuable, believe it or not. Pain helps us to connect with others; it teaches us to be more compassionate and less arrogant and judgmental towards others. When you've been broken, you feel for those who are being broken, and you know how to help them and comfort them because you've been there. So don't waste your time trying to change or cover up the past. Use it. Learn from it and allow it to produce a passion in your heart for others who are in similar situations as those you faced. In fact, that's probably why God let you experience that particular pain—He wanted you to reach others who are in that same situation. Today, I have a burning passion in my heart to help people caught up in the immigration system and locked up in prison. I had no plans on doing this when I was a teenager. When asked what I wanted to be when I was a little girl, I never said I wanted to go into prisons and talk to inmates and immigrants and provide them with hope

CHAPTER 12: CLOSURE

and faith. That was nowhere on my mind. But now, it's my passion. Why? Because it was once my pain. My pain produced my passion and pointed me in the direction of my life's purpose. Trust me when I say, "God causes everything to work together for the good of those who love God and are called according to his purpose" (Romans 8:28, NLT). That especially applies to the painful situations in our lives.

*

I pray my story has been inspiring to you. What I pray most is that it has pointed you in the direction of the God that found me when I was at my lowest point. Close your eyes for a moment and picture a wonderful future that's waiting for you. See it in your mind's eye. You can have it. As long as you're not dead, there's always a chance of a turnaround. Furthermore, when surrendered to God, you will always come out on top in the end. Always! Things that would normally kill you will only make you stronger. Situations that would normally destroy you will only elevate you higher.

Let me pray a simple prayer for you:

Lord Jesus, I surrender my heart and soul to you. Come into my heart and take control of my life. You said you would order my steps and lead me in the right direction, so I'm open to your guidance and I submit to your will. Whatever I'm facing today, I put it in your hands, and I even pray for my enemies that you will open their eyes so that they heed your conviction and find your grace and mercy. I thank

FACE THE MUSIC

you that I'm a winner. All things are currently working out for my good, and no weapon that is formed against me is going to prosper. Thank you, in your name I pray, amen.

ABOUT THE AUTHOR

Antonieta Mitchell is a mother of six children, Lester Thomas jr, Melissa Wharton, Fatimah Ali, Asheley Jackson, Kalia Carew and Amia Carew. She is also a grandmother of seven. She endeavors to be the best mother she can be to her kids and grandkids. She loves to cook - some might even say she's an amazing cook. She loves God and enjoys helping and serving others. Currently, her goal is to speak at immigration detention centers and provide hope to those who are fighting to remain in this country.

To contact author, go to:
Facebook: FaceTheMusic56
Instagram: @ _facethemusic
Email: FaceTheMusic56@gmail.com

www.ingramcontent.com/pod-product-compliance
Lightning Source LLC
LaVergne TN
LVHW041708060526
838201LV00043B/639